# BEANS

SANDRA GLUCK

PHOTOGRAPHY BY

DANA GALLAGHER

CollinsPublishersSanFrancisco

*A Division of* HarperCollins*Publishers*

First published in USA 1995 by Collins Publishers San Francisco
1160 Battery Street, San Francisco, CA 94111

PRODUCED BY SMALLWOOD & STEWART, INC., NEW YORK CITY

© 1995 Smallwood & Stewart, Inc.

EDITOR: David Ricketts
FOOD STYLING: Anne Disrude
BOOK DESIGN: Susi Oberhelman
DESIGN ASSISTANT: Pat Tan

Library of Congress Cataloging-in-Publication Data

Gluck, Sandra.
    Beans / Sandra Gluck.
        p.        cm. — (The gourmet pantry)
    Includes index.
    ISBN 0-00-225026-8
    1. Cookery (Beans) I. Title.    II. Series.
TX803.B4G58            1995
641.6'565—dc20                        95-5950

PRINTED IN ITALY

10  9  8  7  6  5  4  3  2  1

# CONTENTS

# INTRODUCTION

There are hundreds of varieties of pulses—beans, lentils, and peas. Grown in pods, then picked and dried, pulses are actually the seeds of leguminous plants, those plants with nodules on their roots that contain nitrogen-fixing bacteria. Pulses were among mankind's first crops: Soybeans, used today in countless foods, were cultivated in Asia 4,000 years ago, while kidney, pinto, and navy beans date back to 5,000 B.C. This ancient food source has kept many cultures alive through harsh winters and lean times.

With more and more research affirming the need to eat lower on the food chain, we recognize the importance of beans, which provide quality protein without excessive fat. With the exception of soybeans, beans do not supply complete proteins. But pair them with a grain such as rice, and together they make an excellent and inexpensive source of protein.

Beans offer the cook a palette on which to draw. They act as flavor sponges, soaking up the seasonings and nuances of the dish in which they are cooked. They can be combined with other ingredients in almost limitless ways, in soups, stews, casseroles, and salads.

While beans marry easily with other ingredients, they are satisfying in their own right, adorned with only a pinch of a spice or an herb, a splash of lemon juice, or a few drops of fruity olive oil. The bean happily zigzags

from one culture to another, adapting and absorbing the particular flavors of each country. The recipes in this book range from familiar dishes such as hummus, black bean soup, and chili, to more innovative ones, such as red bean ice cream, chocolate bean cake, and white bean pie. As new bean hybrids emerge and heirloom varieties are reborn, feel free to experiment with all kinds of beans, tasting and comparing. There is no right or wrong —the bean is acquiescent. But remember that cooking beans takes some time. The beans in these recipes, with the exception of black beans, need to be presoaked. While the recipes call for soaking overnight, you may also do a quick-soak: In a saucepan, combine the beans with water to cover by 2 inches and bring to a boil for 1 minute. Remove from the heat, cover and let stand for 1 hour. Drain and proceed with the recipe. And please do not add salt when cooking beans—it will toughen their skins.

Many of the newer gourmet packed beans call for cooking without any soaking—follow that direction. Buy your beans in a store that does a brisk business. Fresher beans will cook more evenly and older beans will need more cooking time. All beans should be carefully picked through before cooking, since there are often bits of organic debris lurking about.

The good news is that beans are good for us; the best news is that they taste good, too. Try these recipes and enjoy.

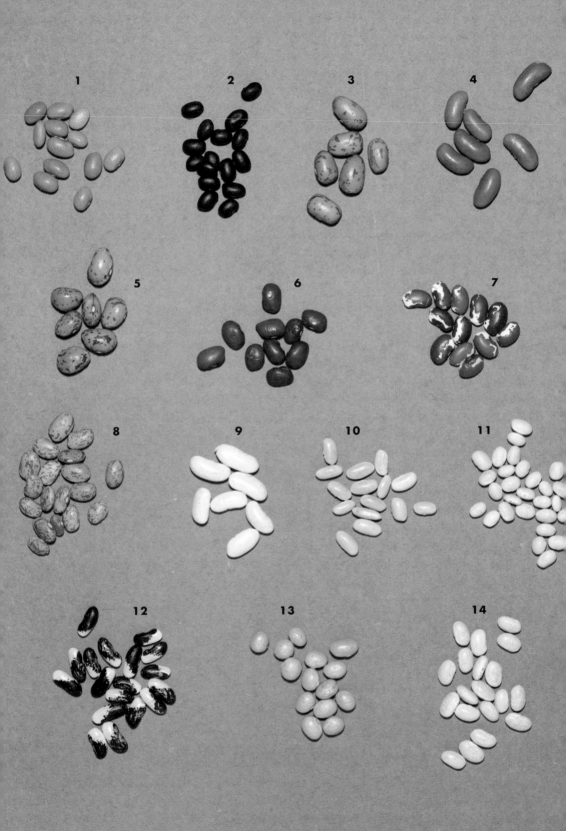

# GLOSSARY

**ADZUKI BEANS** (*azuki*) (19)
Frequently used in Japanese cooking, these small red beans are somewhat sweet, with a soft texture when cooked. They are used in both savory and sweet dishes. There is no substitute.

**ANASAZI BEANS** (7)
Anasazis, considered a white bean, are small and meaty flavored. The name means "ancient ones" in Navajo.

**APPALOOSA BEANS** (12)
A member of the pinto bean family, these small, speckled hybrids are grown in the Palouse region of the American Northwest.

**BLACK BEANS** (*turtle beans*) (2)
These smoky sweet and creamy beans are often paired with hot spices in Central and South American dishes. They do not have to be soaked before cooking.

**BLACK-EYED PEAS** (*Southern peas, brown-eyed peas, crowder peas*) (20)
Dull white with a black spot and slight kidney shape, black-eyed peas become mealy when cooked. Tender and savory, they are the perfect foil for slightly bitter greens and bacon.

**CHICK-PEAS** (*garbanzos, ceci beans*) (24)
Buff colored with a rich nutty flavor, these beans hold up particularly well after cooking. Check to make certain they are cooked to the right degree of tenderness.

**CHINA YELLOW BEANS** (13)
Smooth and round in shape, mellow and silky when cooked, these pale sulphur-yellow beans work well in highly seasoned dishes.

**CRANBERRY BEANS** (*Roman beans*) (3)
These medium-sized red mottled beans have a mild, nutty flavor. Traditionally cranberry beans are paired with limas to make succotash.

**FAVA BEANS** (*broad beans*) (23)
Brownish green in color, and slightly bitter with a granular texture, favas are available both fresh and dried. Always remove the outer skin.

**FLAGEOLETS** (10)
Called the Cadillac of beans because of their higher price, this common French variety is pale green with a delicate flavor. Flageolets are traditionally paired with lamb.

**GIGANDES** (18)
These large white beans imported from Greece and Spain are slightly mealy when cooked. Sweet white runner beans are a good substitute.

**GREAT NORTHERN BEANS** (14)
Small, bright white, and slightly kidney shaped, these beans have a mild flavor and creamy texture similar to white kidney beans.

**KIDNEY BEANS** (4)
These are meaty-flavored and kidney-shaped, with a creamy texture when cooked. They come in red and white varieties.

**LENTILS, BROWN** (17)
A staple of the ancient Greeks and Romans, lentils are mild-flavored and cook to a soft texture. Like other lentils, they do not require any soaking.

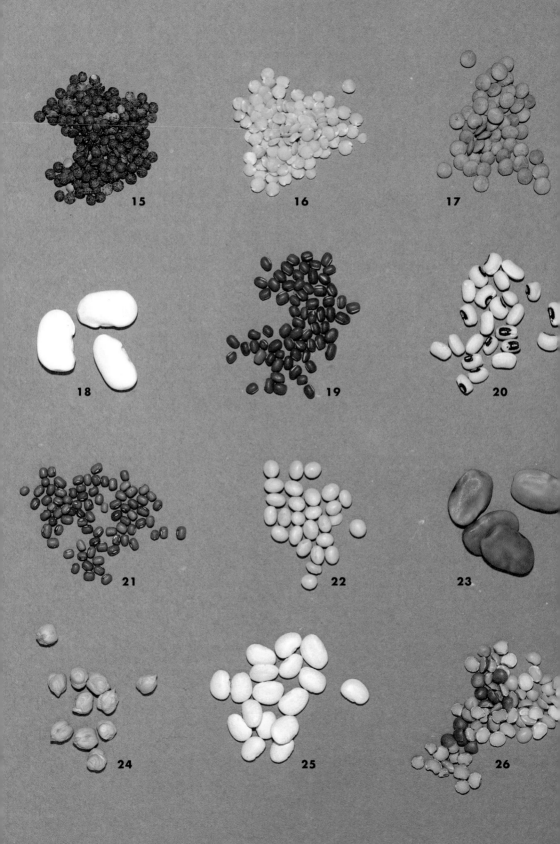

## LENTILS, GREEN (17)

These flat, disk-shaped pulses, ranging from green to golden brown, are protein rich, yet inexpensive. Domestic varieties are not as plump or nutty as their French relatives.

## LENTILS, GREEN FRENCH (15)

Plump and olive green in color, these lentils remain slightly crisp when cooked, with a pronounced nutty flavor. Called LePuy lentils, they are imported from France.

## LENTILS, RED (16)

Bright orange-red, these imported lentils are generally sold split and become very soft when cooked. They are best in purées or soups.

## LIMA BEANS (*butter bean*) (25)

These white beans range in size from ½ inch to 1 inch in length. Savory in flavor and somewhat mealy in texture, they marry well with buttery sauces and robust, piquant dishes. The large lima is starchier than its thinner-skinned cousin, the baby lima.

## MOONG DAL (21)

These hulled mung beans—green, black, brown, or yellow—are a North Indian staple. They are somewhat sweet in flavor and are complemented by hot spices.

## NAVY BEANS (*pea bean*) (11)

Said to have been the favorite beans on navy battleships, these small white beans are mildly flavored and mealy-textured.

## PINK BEANS (1)

Similar to both the pinto bean and the small red chili bean, these brownish-red, uniformly colored beans are long rather than round and are slightly sweet and meaty-flavored.

## PINTO BEANS (8)

Named for the pinto horse whose markings it mimics, these beans are full-flavored with a mealy texture when cooked. When cooked, pinto beans turn a uniform shade of brownish-red. They may be used interchangeably with kidney beans.

## SMALL RED BEANS (*small red chili beans, Red Mexican beans*) (6)

Less than ½ inch in size, these beans are similar in flavor to the kidney bean. They are slightly sweet, with a meaty flavor and creamy texture.

## SOYBEANS (22)

Soybeans are available in a variety of colors, from yellow, green, and brown to black and mottled. They require lengthy cooking, and are firm-textured with a mild flavor when cooked.

## SPLIT PEAS (26)

Both green and yellow, the split form of garden peas are mild-flavored and soft-textured. There is no need for presoaking. They are best in soups and purées.

## STEUBEN YELLOW-EYE BEANS

Mildly flavored with a thin skin, Yellow-Eyes take to long, slow cooking and absorb flavor while the texture becomes creamy and smooth.

## SWEET WHITE RUNNER BEANS

These large beans, kidney-shaped and creamy in texture, hold their own when bathed in highly seasoned, assertive sauces and dressings.

## TONGUES OF FIRE (*Lingua di Fuoco*) (5)

A type of cranberry bean, these medium-size round beans have a sweet and delicate flavor and a creamy texture when cooked.

## WHITE KIDNEY BEANS (*cannellini*) (9)

Mildly flavored, these beans have a creamy texture when cooked. Similar to Great Northern Beans, they are wonderful in salads or simply tossed with oil and vinegar.

# FIVE-BEAN SOUP

THIS IS A PARTICULARLY NICE MIX TO HAVE ON HAND FOR
DISHES THAT USE SEVERAL KINDS OF BEANS. THE FLAVORS, COLORS, AND
TEXTURES OF EACH BEAN COMBINE FOR A MORE INTERESTING
SOUP, WHETHER IT'S THIS ONE OR YOUR OWN FAVORITE RECIPE. STORE
THE MIX TIGHTLY COVERED IN A COOL, DARK PLACE.

**FIVE-BEAN MIX**

½ cup dried black beans, picked
   over & rinsed

½ cup dried small red chili beans,
   picked over & rinsed

⅓ cup dried Great Northern beans,
   picked over & rinsed

⅓ cup dried tongues of fire
   or cranberry beans,
   picked over & rinsed

⅓ cup dried anasazi beans, picked
   over & rinsed

1 tablespoon olive oil

2 large onions, coarsely chopped

6 garlic cloves, minced

2 carrots, quartered lengthwise
   & thinly sliced crosswise

2 cups chopped ripe tomatoes or
   canned crushed tomatoes

½ cup finely chopped fresh basil

1 teaspoon salt

In a large bowl, soak the beans overnight in water to cover by 3 inches. Drain and set the beans aside.

In a large nonreactive Dutch oven or casserole, heat the oil over medium-low heat. Add the onions and garlic, and cook, stirring frequently, for about 7 minutes, or until softened. Stir in the carrots and cook, stirring frequently, for about 5 minutes, or until tender. Stir in the tomatoes and basil and cook for 3 minutes.

Add 8 cups water and the beans and bring to a boil over medium heat, skimming any foam that rises to the surface. Reduce the heat, partially cover, and simmer, stirring occasionally, for about 1½ hours, or until the beans are tender.

Stir the salt into the soup and ladle into warmed soup bowls.

# BLACK BEAN SOUP

SERVES 4

YEARS AGO WHILE WORKING WITH COOKBOOK
AUTHOR JEAN ANDERSON, I WAS SURPRISED TO FIND THAT SHE
COOKED BLACK BEANS WITHOUT PRIOR SOAKING, A
METHOD SHARED WITH HER BY KATHY KAGEL, THE CHEF-OWNER
OF CAFÉ PASQUAL IN SANTA FE.

In a large nonreactive Dutch oven or heavy-bottomed saucepan, heat the oil over medium heat. Add the onions and cook, stirring frequently, for about 20 minutes, or until they are golden brown and caramelized. Add the garlic and fresh ginger, and cook for 2 to 3 minutes, or until the garlic is softened and aromatic.

Stir in the leek, bell pepper, and jalapeño, and cook, stirring frequently, for about 7 minutes, or until the vegetables are softened. Stir in the tomatoes and cook, stirring frequently, for about 5 minutes, or until all the liquid has evaporated.

Stir in the beans, sweet potato, boiling potato, broth, ground ginger, salt, pepper, and cayenne. Bring to a boil, skimming any foam that rises to the surface. Reduce the heat, and simmer, covered, for about 1 hour, or until the beans are tender.

Working in batches if necessary, transfer the bean mixture to a food processor fitted with the metal blade and process until smooth. Pour into a medium-mesh sieve placed over a bowl and push the solids through with the back of a spoon. Return the soup to the pot and gently reheat over low heat, stirring. Stir in the sherry and ladle into warmed serving bowls.

¼ cup olive oil

2 medium-size onions, coarsely chopped

5 garlic cloves, minced

1 tablespoon minced peeled fresh ginger

1 leek, halved lengthwise & thinly sliced

1 large green bell pepper, cored, seeded & diced

1 jalapeño, cored, seeded & sliced

1 pound ripe tomatoes, peeled & coarsely chopped, or 2 cups canned crushed tomatoes

1½ cups dried black beans, picked over & rinsed

1 sweet potato, peeled & thinly sliced

1 boiling potato, peeled & thinly sliced

5½ cups chicken broth

½ teaspoon ground ginger

1 teaspoon salt

¼ teaspoon freshly ground black pepper

¼ teaspoon cayenne

2 tablespoons dry sherry

# CORN & BEAN CHOWDER
# WITH ROASTED RED PEPPER

S E R V E S   4

CHICKEN BROTH INFUSED WITH THE RICH FLAVOR OF CORN

IS THE BASE FOR THIS CREAMY CHOWDER, PERFECT FOR EARLY AUTUMN

SUPPERS. IF YOU LIKE, PREPARE THE SOUP IN STAGES, COOKING

THE BROTH AND THE BEANS AND ROASTING THE PEPPERS IN ADVANCE,

THEN COMBINING ALL THE ELEMENTS JUST BEFORE SERVING.

¾ cup dried navy beans, China yellow beans, or black-eyed peas, picked over & rinsed

2 garlic cloves, minced

1 teaspoon dried marjoram

3 ears corn, husked, kernels scraped off, corn & cobs reserved

4 cups chicken broth

2 red bell peppers, cored, seeded & halved

2 teaspoons olive oil

2 ounces smoked bacon, diced

2 green bell peppers, cored, seeded & coarsely chopped

¾ cup minced green onions

1 tablespoon plus 1 teaspoon all-purpose flour

⅔ cup milk

½ teaspoon salt

¼ teaspoon cayenne

In a large bowl, soak the beans or peas overnight in water to cover by 3 inches. Drain.

In a medium-size saucepan, combine the beans or peas with water to cover by 3 inches. Bring to a boil, skimming any foam that rises to the surface. Reduce the heat and stir in the garlic and marjoram. Partially cover and simmer for about 1 hour, or until the beans or peas are tender; stir occasionally and add water if necessary to keep the beans or peas covered. Drain, reserving ½ cup of the cooking liquid. Set the beans aside.

Cut the corn cobs in half. In a large saucepan, combine the broth and the cobs and bring to a boil over medium heat. Reduce the heat and simmer, covered, for 35 minutes, or until the broth is full of corn flavor. Strain the broth and set aside. Discard the cobs.

Preheat the broiler, with the pan 6 inches from the heat source. Place the red bell peppers skin side up on the pan and broil for about 10 minutes, or until the skin is charred and blistered. Place the peppers in a paper bag, close the bag, and let cool. Peel the red bell peppers and dice.

In a large saucepan or Dutch oven, heat the oil over medium heat. Add the bacon and cook for about 4 minutes, or until slightly crisp. With a slotted spoon, remove the bacon to paper towels to

drain. Add the green bell peppers and green onions to the saucepan and cook, stirring frequently, for about 6 minutes, or until the peppers are tender. Stir in the flour until the vegetables are well coated, then gradually stir in the reserved corn broth and the milk. Stir in the beans or peas and the reserved ½ cup bean cooking liquid, the salt, and cayenne. Bring to a boil, reduce the heat, and simmer, stirring occasionally, for about 5 minutes, or until the chowder is slightly thickened. Stir in the bacon, the corn kernels with any liquid, and the diced red bell pepper and cook for 2 to 3 minutes, or until the corn is just tender. Ladle into warmed serving bowls.

# MINTED SPLIT PEA SOUP

SERVES 4

THIS IS A VARIATION ON THE CLASSIC FRENCH
SOUP, WHICH USES FRESH SPRING PEAS. HERE THE PEA SOUP
IS LIGHTENED BY THE ADDITION OF LETTUCE
LEAVES DURING THE FINAL STAGE OF COOKING. FOR A
SUMMER REFRESHER, SERVE THE SOUP CHILLED.

1 tablespoon plus 1 teaspoon
   olive oil

1 cup chopped onions

2 green onions, thinly sliced

3 garlic cloves, minced

2 tablespoons chopped peeled
   fresh ginger

1 carrot, thinly sliced

1 cup green split peas, yellow
   split peas, or brown lentils,
   picked over & rinsed

½ cup packed fresh mint leaves

3 cups chicken broth

¾ teaspoon salt

¼ teaspoon grated nutmeg

3 cups torn Boston lettuce leaves

⅓ cup heavy cream

In a large heavy-bottomed saucepan or Dutch oven, heat the oil over low heat. Add the onions, green onions, garlic, and ginger and cook, stirring frequently, for about 10 minutes, or until softened.

Stir in the carrot and cook, stirring frequently, for 5 minutes, or until the carrot is almost tender. Stir in the peas or lentils and mint. Stir in the broth, 1½ cups water, the salt, and nutmeg, and bring to a boil over medium heat. Reduce the heat, cover, and simmer, stirring occasionally, for about 40 minutes, or until the peas or lentils are tender. Stir in the lettuce and cook for 5 minutes, or until the lettuce has wilted and softened.

Working in batches if necessary, transfer the soup to a food processor fitted with the metal blade and process until smooth. Return the soup to the saucepan, stir in the cream, and gently reheat, stirring. Ladle into warmed serving bowls.

# TUSCAN BEAN SOUP

SERVES 4

A CRANBERRY-TYPE BEAN NATIVE TO ITALY, TONGUES OF
FIRE HAVE A SWEET, FRESH TASTE WITH A MEATY TEXTURE, AND LIKE
MANY BEANS, THEY ABSORB FLAVORS WELL. TOPPED WITH CRISP
PARMESAN TOASTS, THIS HEARTY SOUP COULD BE A MAIN DISH. DURING
THE WARMER MONTHS, SERVE IT AT ROOM TEMPERATURE.

In a large bowl, soak the beans overnight in water to cover by 3 inches. Drain.

In a large pot, combine the beans with water to cover by 3 inches. Bring to a boil over medium heat, skimming foam that rises to the surface. Reduce the heat, partially cover, and simmer 10 minutes. Drain.

In a large Dutch oven or heavy-bottomed saucepan, heat the oil over medium heat. Add the bacon and cook for about 4 minutes, or until lightly crisped. With a slotted spoon, remove the bacon to paper towels to drain. Add the onion and garlic to the pot and cook, stirring frequently, for about 7 minutes, or until softened. Add the bell pepper and carrots and cook, stirring occasionally, for about 7 minutes, or until softened. Stir in the tomato. Add 4 cups water, broth, beans, and bacon, and bring to a boil. Reduce the heat, cover, and simmer for 45 minutes, or until the beans are tender.

Return the soup to a boil. Stir in the celeriac, kale, pasta, and salt, and cook for 10 minutes longer, or until the pasta and vegetables are tender.

Meanwhile, prepare the toasts: Preheat the broiler, with the rack 6 inches from the heat. Brush the bread with the olive oil and sprinkle with the Parmesan. Broil for 3 to 4 minutes, or until the cheese is golden brown and the bread is crisp. Ladle the soup into large bowls and top each with toast.

¾ cup dried tongues of fire, cranberry or cannellini beans, picked over & rinsed

2 teaspoons olive oil

4 ounces sliced bacon, diced

1 large onion, coarsely chopped

4 garlic cloves, minced

1 large red bell pepper, cored, seeded & cut into ½-inch dice

2 carrots, quartered lengthwise & thinly sliced crosswise

1 large ripe tomato, peeled & coarsely chopped

2 cups chicken broth

1 celeriac, peeled & cut into ½-inch dice

1 bunch kale, stemmed & coarsely chopped (about 6 cups)

½ cup small pasta shapes, such as squares or elbows

¾ teaspoon salt

PARMESAN TOASTS

12 pieces crusty French peasant or Italian bread, about 2½ by 1½ by ½ inch

2 tablespoons plus 2 teaspoons olive oil

¼ cup freshly grated Parmesan cheese

*Tuscan Bean Soup (overleaf)*

# UKRAINIAN BORSCHT

BORSCHT RECIPES ABOUND, FROM MEATLESS DISHES TO
EARTHY AFFAIRS FULL OF VEGETABLES, MEAT, AND BEANS. THE UKRAINIAN
VERSION TYPICALLY CONTAINS MEAT, AND HERE WE
ALSO TOSS IN ROAST BEEF BONES AND VEGETABLES TO FLAVOR THE BROTH
MORE FULLY. THE LIMA BEANS ADD CREAMINESS AND BODY.

½ cup dried baby or large
  lima beans, picked
  over & rinsed

2 pounds beef bones

1¼ pounds beef chuck,
  in one piece

2 large carrots, halved

1 large parsnip, peeled & cut up

1 large turnip, peeled & cut up

1 large onion, unpeeled & halved

2½ cups tomato-vegetable juice

2 beets, peeled & cut up

½ small head cabbage, cut into
  1-inch chunks

2 medium-size boiling potatoes,
  peeled & cut into
  1-inch chunks

½ cup snipped fresh dill

3 tablespoons red wine vinegar

¼ teaspoon ground allspice

1 teaspoon salt

½ teaspoon freshly ground
  black pepper

In a large bowl, soak the beans overnight in water to cover by 3 inches. Drain and set aside. Preheat the oven to 450°F.

Place the beef bones, chuck, carrots, parsnip, turnip, and onion in a large baking pan and roast, stirring occasionally, for about 45 minutes, or until browned. Transfer to a large Dutch oven or soup pot and add 8 cups cold water and tomato-vegetable juice. Bring to a boil over high heat, skimming any foam that rises to the surface; reduce the heat and simmer, partially covered, for 2 hours. Remove the bones and vegetables with a slotted spoon and discard.

Add the beans and beets to the pot. Return to a boil, reduce the heat, and simmer, partially covered, for 45 minutes, or until beans are almost tender. Add the cabbage and potatoes and simmer, partially covered, for 15 minutes, or until the potatoes are tender. Stir in the dill, vinegar, allspice, salt, and pepper.

To serve, remove the beef with tongs or a fork to a cutting surface and thinly slice. Divide the meat among warmed serving bowls and ladle in the soup.

# VIETNAMESE CHICKEN SOUP
# WITH BLACK-EYED PEAS

SERVES 4

SALTY AND AROMATIC FISH SAUCE, TART
TAMARIND PASTE, AND FRESH CILANTRO GIVE THIS SOUP
A SWEET, TANGY FLAVOR THAT IS DISTINCTLY
VIETNAMESE. SERVE IT AS A MAIN DISH, ACCOMPANIED BY
A CRISP, REFRESHING CUCUMBER SALAD.

In a large bowl, soak the peas or beans overnight in water to cover by 3 inches. Drain.

In a medium-size pot, combine the peas or beans with water to cover by 3 inches. Bring to a boil over medium heat, skimming any foam that rises to the surface. Reduce the heat, partially cover, and simmer for 45 minutes to 1 hour, or until the peas or beans are tender; stir occasionally and add water if necessary to keep the peas or beans covered. Drain and set the peas or beans aside.

In a large nonreactive Dutch oven or casserole, heat the oil over low heat. Add the green onions, garlic, and ginger, and cook, stirring frequently, for about 4 minutes, or until the green onions are softened. Increase the heat to medium, stir in the tomatoes, and cook for 2 minutes, or until the mixture has lost some of its moisture. Add the broth, fish sauce, tamarind mixture, and lemongrass, and bring to a boil.

Stir in the peas or beans, chicken, mushrooms, and capellini. Return to a boil and boil gently for about 5 minutes, or until the chicken and pasta are cooked and the mushrooms are tender. Stir in the cilantro and basil and ladle into warmed bowls.

¾ cup dried black-eyed peas, navy beans, or China yellow beans, picked over & rinsed

2 teaspoons peanut oil

3 green onions, thinly sliced

6 garlic cloves, minced

2 tablespoons minced peeled fresh ginger

½ cup chopped ripe tomatoes or canned crushed tomatoes

5 cups chicken broth

1 tablespoon Vietnamese or Thai fish sauce, such as nuoc mam or nam plo

1 teaspoon tamarind paste, dissolved in 1 tablespoon hot water

1 tablespoon chopped fresh lemongrass or 1 teaspoon ground dried

12 ounces skinless, boneless chicken thighs, cut into 1-inch chunks

10 ounces fresh shiitake mushrooms, stemmed & sliced ¼ inch thick

3 ounces capellini, broken into 2-inch lengths

¼ cup minced fresh cilantro

¼ cup minced fresh basil

*Vietnamese Chicken Soup*
*with Black-Eyed Peas (overleaf)*

# HUMMUS

MAKES 1 1/2 CUPS

IN THIS VERSION OF HUMMUS, DARK ASIAN SESAME OIL AND
ROASTED GARLIC REPLACE THE MORE TRADITIONAL SESAME PASTE. THIS
IS AN INSTANCE WHERE CANNED CHICK-PEAS WORK AS WELL AS
COOKED DRIED ONES. SERVE HUMMUS AS A SPREAD WITH PITA BREAD
OR GENOA TOAST OR AS A DIP WITH RAW VEGETABLES.

If using dried chick-peas, soak them in a large bowl overnight in water to cover by 3 inches. Drain. In a medium-size saucepan, combine the chick-peas with water to cover by 3 inches. Bring to a boil over medium heat. Reduce the heat, skimming any foam that rises to the surface, and simmer, partially covered, for about 1½ hours, or until tender; stir occasionally and add water if necessary to keep the chick-peas covered. Drain and set aside.

Meanwhile, preheat the oven to 450°F. Wrap the garlic head in foil, place on a small baking sheet, and roast for about 40 minutes, or until the garlic pulp is soft. When cool enough to handle, cut off the stem end and squeeze the soft garlic pulp from the skins into a measuring cup. Discard the skins. You should have about ⅓ cup garlic pulp.

In a food processor fitted with the metal blade, combine the chick-peas, roasted garlic, and sesame oil, and process for about 30 seconds, or until puréed. Add the sour cream, lemon juice, paprika, allspice, salt, and cayenne and process until smooth. Hummus will keep, covered, in the refrigerator for up to 3 days.

½ cup dried chick-peas, picked over & rinsed, or 1 (19 ounce) can chick-peas, rinsed & drained

1 whole head garlic, unpeeled

2 tablespoons dark Asian sesame oil

¼ cup light sour cream

2 teaspoons fresh lemon juice

¼ teaspoon sweet paprika

⅛ teaspoon ground allspice

¾ teaspoon salt

⅛ teaspoon cayenne

# WHITE BEANS WITH SKORDALIA

SERVES 4

SKORDALIA, THE THICK AND LEMONY GREEK
SAUCE, IS MADE WITH POTATOES, GARLIC, AND OLIVE OIL,
THEN COMBINED WITH FLESHY WHITE BEANS.
SERVED WITH CRISP, OLIVE OIL-SOAKED BREAD, THE
COMBINATION IS A MEAL IN ITSELF.

¾ cup dried gigandes,
    sweet white runners,
    or large lima beans, picked
    over & rinsed

2 garlic cloves, peeled

½ teaspoon minced fresh oregano

SKORDALIA

1 boiling potato (about 4 ounces),
    peeled & thinly sliced

2 garlic cloves, peeled

2 tablespoons extra-virgin olive oil

1 tablespoon fresh lemon juice

½ teaspoon salt

½ teaspoon minced fresh oregano

Fresh oregano sprigs, for garnish
    (optional)

Lemon wedges (optional)

In a medium-size bowl, soak the beans overnight in water to cover by 3 inches. Drain.

In a medium-size saucepan, combine the beans, garlic, oregano, and water to cover by 3 inches. Bring to a boil over medium heat, skimming any foam that rises to the surface. Reduce the heat and simmer, partially covered for about 1½ hours, or until the beans are tender; stir occasionally and add water if necessary to keep the beans covered. Drain and set aside.

Meanwhile, prepare the skordalia: In a medium-size saucepan, combine the potato and lightly salted water to cover. Bring to a boil over high heat and cook for about 10 minutes, or until tender, adding the garlic during the last minute of cooking. Drain, reserving 3 tablespoons of the cooking liquid.

With an electric mixer at low speed, beat the potatoes and garlic until smooth. Beat in the oil, lemon juice, salt, and the reserved cooking liquid until creamy.

To serve, transfer the beans to a serving bowl, spoon the skordalia over, and toss gently to combine. Sprinkle with the minced oregano and garnish with oregano sprigs and lemon wedges if desired.

# FAVA PURÉE
# WITH GARLIC & LEMON

MAKES 2 CUPS

SWEET FENNEL SEEDS NICELY COMPLEMENT THE SLIGHTLY
BITTER FAVA BEAN PURÉE, AND FRUITY EXTRA-VIRGIN OLIVE OIL
ADDS A REMARKABLE SILKINESS. SERVE THIS RICH SPREAD
AS PART OF AN APPETIZER PLATE, ALONG WITH GRILLED BREAD
OR FOCACCIA AND ASSORTED VEGETABLES.

1 generous cup dried fava beans,
  picked over & rinsed

6 garlic cloves, peeled

1 teaspoon dried oregano

1 bay leaf, preferably Turkish

¼ teaspoon fennel seeds

¼ cup extra-virgin olive oil

1 tablespoon hazelnut oil

3 tablespoons fresh lemon juice

½ teaspoon salt

⅛ teaspoon cayenne

2 tablespoons snipped fresh dill

In a large bowl, soak the beans overnight in water to cover by 3 inches. Drain.

In a medium-size saucepan, combine the beans with water to cover by 3 inches. Bring to a boil over medium heat, skimming any foam that rises to the surface. Reduce the heat and simmer, partially covered, for 15 minutes. Drain the beans and rinse out the saucepan.

With your fingers or a paring knife, peel and discard the tough outer skin from the beans and discard. Return the beans to the saucepan along with the garlic, oregano, bay leaf, fennel seeds, and water to cover by 3 inches. Bring to a boil. Reduce the heat, partially cover, and simmer, for about 25 minutes, or until the beans are very tender; stir occasionally and add water if necessary to keep the beans covered. Drain and discard the bay leaf.

Place the favas and garlic in a food processor fitted with the metal blade and process until puréed. Add the olive oil, hazelnut oil, lemon juice, salt, and cayenne, and process until smooth. Transfer to a serving bowl and stir in the dill. Serve at room temperature. Covered, the purée will keep in the refrigerator for several days; bring to room temperature before serving.

# THREE-BEAN SALAD

A MEMBER OF THE PINTO FAMILY, THE APPALOOSA BEAN
IS A GORGEOUS HYBRID, CREAMY WHITE WITH AN IRREGULAR BLACK
MARKING. THE SMALLER PINK BEAN IS SLIGHTLY SWEET
AND MEATY, WHILE THE CHINA YELLOW IS LESS ASSERTIVE IN FLAVOR,
A GOOD PARTNER FOR THE OIL AND VINEGAR DRESSING.

In a large bowl, soak the beans overnight in enough water to cover by 3 inches. Drain.

In a medium-size saucepan, combine the beans with enough water to cover by 3 inches. Bring to a boil over medium heat, skimming any foam that rises to the surface. Reduce the heat, partially cover, and simmer, for about 1 hour, or until the beans are tender; stir occasionally and add water if necessary to keep the beans covered. Drain and set aside.

Meanwhile, in a large pot of boiling salted water, cook the potatoes for about 10 minutes, or until just tender. Drain.

In a large bowl, whisk together the oil, vinegar, and salt. Set aside.

Add the potatoes along with the beans to the dressing in the bowl. Fold in the tomato, celery, cucumber, mint, and green onion. Serve at room temperature.

⅓ cup dried appaloosa beans, picked over & rinsed

⅓ cup dried pink beans, picked over & rinsed

⅓ cup dried China yellow beans, picked over & rinsed

2 boiling potatoes, peeled & cut into ½-inch dice

3 tablespoons extra-virgin olive oil

2 tablespoons balsamic vinegar

½ teaspoon salt

1 large ripe tomato, peeled & diced

1 celery stalk, cut into ¼-inch dice

1 kirby cucumber, peeled, seeded & cut into ¼-inch dice

¼ cup chopped fresh mint

1 green onion, thinly sliced

# GREEN LENTILS & SPINACH
# WITH FETA CHEESE & PECANS

SERVES 4

COOKED IN TOMATO-VEGETABLE JUICE

AND CHICKEN BROTH, THESE GREEN LENTILS ARE FULL

OF FLAVOR, TENDER, YET SLIGHTLY CRUNCHY.

IF YOU PREFER, BROWN LENTILS CAN FILL IN

FOR THE GREEN ONES.

Preheat the oven to 350°F.

In a small bowl, cover the feta with cold water and let stand for 15 minutes to remove the saltiness. Drain well. Crumble the feta and set aside.

Meanwhile, place the pecans on a baking sheet and toast in the oven, stirring occasionally, for about 7 minutes, or until crisp and fragrant. Let cool, then coarsely chop.

In a medium-size saucepan, combine the broth and garlic and bring to a boil over medium heat. Add the lentils, reduce the heat and simmer, covered, for 20 minutes. Stir in the tomato-vegetable juice, carrots, and green onions. Return to a boil, reduce the heat and simmer, covered, for 10 minutes, or until the lentils are tender but not mushy and almost all the liquid has been absorbed. Remove from the heat.

In a large bowl, whisk together the olive oil, walnut oil, vinegar, salt, and pepper. Add the lentil mixture, tossing to coat. Gently fold in the tomatoes and feta. Place the spinach on 4 serving plates, spoon the salad on top, and sprinkle with the nuts.

4 ounces feta cheese

½ cup pecan halves

2¼ cups chicken broth

2 garlic cloves, minced

1 cup French green lentils, picked over & rinsed

½ cup tomato-vegetable juice

3 medium-size carrots, cut into small dice

2 green onions, thinly sliced

1 tablespoon extra-virgin olive oil

2 teaspoons walnut oil

1 tablespoon balsamic vinegar

½ teaspoon salt

¼ teaspoon freshly ground black pepper

1½ cups cherry tomatoes, halved

4 cups spinach leaves, stemmed

# RED LENTIL, POTATO & CHICK-PEA SALAD WITH CHUTNEY

WHILE CHICK-PEAS NEED CONSIDERABLE TIME TO COOK BEFORE THEY BECOME TENDER, RED LENTILS REQUIRE JUST A FEW MINUTES. BUT DO MAKE THE EFFORT TO USE DRIED CHICK-PEAS; CANNED ONES JUST AREN'T AS GOOD IN THIS RECIPE. DRESSED IN A SPICY YOGURT WITH CHOPPED MANGO CHUTNEY, THIS SALAD IS SMOOTH AND TANGY.

¾ cup dried chick-peas, picked over & rinsed

3 garlic cloves, minced

1 teaspoon ground ginger

2 teaspoons ground turmeric

½ teaspoon salt

2 medium-size boiling potatoes, peeled & cut into ½-inch chunks

½ cup dried red lentils, picked over & rinsed

¾ cup plain low-fat yogurt

2 tablespoons olive oil

2 tablespoons finely chopped mango chutney

1 tablespoon fresh lemon juice

1 teaspoon Dijon mustard

½ cup chopped fresh cilantro

2 green onions, sliced, plus additional for garnish (optional)

1 large Granny Smith apple, cored & cut into ½-inch chunks

In a large bowl, soak the chick-peas overnight in water to cover by 3 inches. Drain.

In a medium-size saucepan, combine the chick-peas with water to cover by 3 inches. Bring to a boil over medium heat, skimming any foam that rises to the surface. Stir in the garlic and ginger. Reduce the heat, partially cover, and simmer for about 1½ hours, or until the chick-peas are tender; stir occasionally and add water if necessary to keep the chick-peas covered. Drain and set the chick-peas aside.

In a large pot, bring 4 cups water to a boil. Add the turmeric and salt. Add the potatoes, return to a boil, and cook for 5 minutes. Add the lentils and cook for 5 minutes longer, or until the potatoes and lentils are tender. Drain.

In a large bowl, whisk together the yogurt, olive oil, chutney, lemon juice, and mustard. Fold in the cilantro, green onions, apple, chick-peas, and potato-lentil mixture. Serve at room temperature garnished with chopped green onions, if desired.

# THAI CHICKEN & NOODLE SALAD WITH ADZUKI BEANS

SERVES 4

COLORFUL, TASTY, AND HEALTHFUL,
THAI COOKING IS FINALLY ENJOYING THE POPULARITY
IT DESERVES. IN THIS MILDLY SPICED
NOODLE SALAD, ADZUKI BEANS, SMALL AND SWEET,
BALANCE THE FLAVORS.

In a large bowl, soak the beans overnight in water to cover by 3 inches. Drain.

In a medium-size saucepan, combine the beans with water to cover by 3 inches. Bring to a boil over medium heat, skimming any foam that rises to the surface. Reduce the heat, partially cover, and simmer, for about 1 hour, or until tender; stir occasionally and add water if necessary to keep the beans covered. Drain and set the beans aside.

Cook the linguine according to the package directions until al dente, firm but tender. Drain. Toss the hot linguine with the oil.

Preheat the broiler, with the pan 6 inches from the heat source. In a large bowl, whisk together the lime juice, fish sauce, tomato paste, 2 tablespoons water, the sugar, and chile paste. Rub 2 tablespoons of the mixture over the chicken breast halves. Broil the chicken for about 5 minutes per side, or until well browned and no longer pink in the center.

Meanwhile, add the beans, carrot, bell pepper, tomatoes, and linguine to the remaining lime juice mixture and toss well to combine. Spoon onto serving plates.

Slice the chicken on the diagonal and arrange on the noodles. Sprinkle with the green onions and peanuts, and garnish with the lime wedges, if desired.

½ cup dried adzuki, black, or small red chili beans, picked over & rinsed

6 ounces linguine

1 tablespoon dark Asian sesame oil

¼ cup fresh lime juice

2 tablespoons Thai or Vietnamese fish sauce, such as *nuoc nam* or *nam pla*

2 tablespoons tomato paste

1½ teaspoons sugar

¾ teaspoon Asian chile paste

4 skinless, boneless chicken breast halves (about 5 ounces each)

1 large carrot, cut into 2- by ¼-inch julienne

1 large red bell pepper, cored, seeded & sliced

1 cup ripe cherry tomatoes, halved

4 green onions, thinly sliced

¼ cup coarsely chopped unsalted peanuts

Lime wedges, for garnish (optional)

# GRILLED FRESH TUNA & WHITE BEAN SALAD

SERVES 4

MELLOW, SMOOTH CANNELLINI BEANS SOAK UP

THE PIQUANT ANCHOVY, RED WINE VINEGAR, AND SAGE DRESSING.

IF YOU LIKE, SUBSTITUTE SWORDFISH FOR THE

TUNA AND WHEN WEATHER PERMITS, GRILL BOTH THE FISH

AND VEGETABLES FOR ADDED FLAVOR.

¾ cup dried cannellini, Great Northern, tongues of fire, or cranberry beans, picked over & rinsed

2 garlic cloves, minced

1 bay leaf, preferably Turkish

½ cup olive oil

¼ cup red wine vinegar

2 canned anchovy fillets, mashed, or 1 teaspoon anchovy paste

1 tablespoon chopped fresh sage or 1 teaspoon dried

2 teaspoons sugar

½ teaspoon salt

1 large red bell pepper, cored, seeded & cut into strips

1 medium-size red onion, cut into ¾-inch chunks

1 medium-size zucchini, halved lengthwise & sliced crosswise ¼ inch thick

8 shiitake or white button mushrooms, stemmed, trimmed & halved if large

1 pound fresh tuna steaks, 1 inch thick

1 Belgian endive, sliced crosswise into thick pieces

In a medium-size bowl, soak the beans overnight in water to cover by 3 inches. Drain.

In a medium-size saucepan, combine the beans with water to cover by 3 inches. Bring to a boil over medium heat, skimming any foam that rises to the surface. Stir in the garlic and bay leaf. Reduce the heat, partially cover, and simmer, for about 1 hour, or until the beans are tender; stir occasionally and add water if necessary to keep the beans covered. Drain and discard the bay leaf. Set the beans aside.

In a large bowl, whisk together the oil, vinegar, anchovy, sage, sugar, and salt. Combine the bell pepper, onion, zucchini, and mushrooms in a second large bowl. Spoon ¼ cup of the dressing over and toss to coat.

Preheat the broiler, with the pan 6 inches from the heat source. Place the vegetables on the broiler pan turning occasionally, for about 5 minutes, or until crisp-tender and slightly charred. Set aside.

Place the tuna on the broiler pan, spoon 2 tablespoons of the dressing over the tuna, and broil, turning once, for 5 minutes, or until medium-rare.

Add the beans, vegetables, and endive to the remaining dressing and toss well. Spoon onto warmed serving plates. Cut the tuna into ½-inch-wide strips and arrange over the vegetables.

# SHRIMP SALAD WITH
# RED CHILI BEANS

SERVES 4

MARINATED SHRIMP EMERGE SUCCULENT AND TENDER AFTER
A BRIEF COOKING IN THIS DISH. COMBINED WITH CRIMSON RED BEANS AND
BATHED IN A TROPICAL DRESSING, THEY MAKE A LUSTROUS
AND REFRESHING SALAD. UNSWEETENED COCONUT MILK CAN BE FOUND IN
SOME SUPERMARKETS AND IN SPECIALTY AND ASIAN FOOD SHOPS.

½ cup dried red chili, black,
  or adzuki beans, picked
  over & rinsed

2 teaspoons sweet paprika

1 teaspoon sugar

Pinch of salt plus ¼ teaspoon

12 ounces large shrimp, peeled
  & deveined

3 tablespoons fresh lime juice

3 tablespoons unsweetened
  coconut milk

2 teaspoons olive oil

⅓ cup chopped fresh cilantro

3 tablespoons chopped fresh mint

1 mango, peeled, pitted & cut
  into chunks

1 medium-size cucumber,
  peeled, seeded & cut
  into sticks

1 small red onion,
  halved & slivered

I n a large bowl, soak the beans overnight in water to cover by 3 inches. Drain.

In a medium-size saucepan, combine the beans with water to cover by 3 inches. Bring to a boil over medium heat, skimming any foam that rises to the surface. Reduce the heat, partially cover, and simmer, for about 1 hour, or until the beans are tender; stir occasionally and add water if necessary to keep the beans covered. Drain and set the beans aside.

In a medium-size bowl, stir together the paprika, sugar, and the pinch of salt. Add the shrimp, tossing well to coat. Let marinate for 30 minutes at room temperature.

Preheat the broiler, with the pan 6 inches from the heat source. Place the shrimp on the broiler pan and broil for about 3 minutes per side, or until pink and opaque in the center. Remove from the heat.

In a large bowl, whisk together the lime juice, coconut milk, oil, cilantro, mint, and the remaining ¼ teaspoon salt. Add the mango, cucumber, onion, beans, and shrimp, along with any juices that have accumulated in the pan. Toss gently to combine. Spoon onto warmed serving plates.

# SWEET POTATO & RED BEAN SALAD
# WITH HAM & GINGER

SERVES 4

SMALL RED CHILI BEANS, AVAILABLE AT THE
SUPERMARKET IN ONE-POUND BAGS, MAINTAIN THEIR COLOR AND
SHAPE BEST WHEN GENTLY COOKED. SPIKED WITH
GINGER JUICE AND MUSTARD, THIS BRACING SALAD MAKES A
DELICIOUS APPETIZER OR LUNCHEON ENTRÉE.

⅓ cup dried small red chili,
    cranberry, tongues of fire,
    or anasazi beans,
    picked over & rinsed

1 large sweet potato
    (about 8 ounces)

1 (3-inch) piece fresh ginger,
    unpeeled

2 tablespoons extra-virgin olive oil

1 tablespoon plus 1 teaspoon
    red wine vinegar

1 teaspoon Dijon mustard

½ teaspoon sugar

⅛ teaspoon ground allspice

⅛ teaspoon grated nutmeg

½ teaspoon salt

½ teaspoon freshly ground
    black pepper

1 small red onion, halved
    lengthwise & thinly
    sliced crosswise

2 ounces baked ham, cut into
    2- by ½-inch julienne

2 cups arugula leaves

In a medium-size bowl, soak the beans overnight in water to cover by 3 inches. Drain.

In a medium-size saucepan, combine the beans with water to cover by 3 inches. Bring to a boil, skimming any foam that rises to the surface. Reduce the heat and simmer, partially covered, for about 1 hour, or until the beans are tender; stir occasionally and add water if necessary to keep the beans covered. Drain and set aside.

Meanwhile, preheat the oven to 425°F. Place the sweet potato on a baking sheet and gently prick the skin in several places. Bake for about 1 hour, or until fork-tender. Let cool, then peel, and cut into 1-inch cubes.

While the potato bakes, grate the ginger over a small bowl with a vegetable grater. With your hands, squeeze the ginger pulp to extract as much juice as possible. Discard the pulp. You should have about 2 tablespoons of juice. Pour the juice into a large bowl and whisk in the oil, vinegar, mustard, sugar, allspice, nutmeg, salt, and pepper. Add the onion, tossing to coat, and let stand for 10 minutes.

Add the beans, ham, and sweet potato to the ginger dressing and toss gently to coat. Just before serving, add the arugula and toss gently to combine.

# HOPPIN' JOHN

IN THE SOUTH, EATING A STEAMING BOWL OF THE
BLACK-EYED PEA AND RICE DISH CALLED HOPPIN' JOHN ON NEW
YEAR'S DAY IS SAID TO BRING GOOD LUCK FOR THE YEAR
AHEAD. ANDOUILLE, A HOT, HIGHLY SEASONED SAUSAGE, IS AVAILABLE
FROM MAIL-ORDER SOURCES AND SOME BUTCHER SHOPS.

In a medium-size bowl, soak the peas overnight in water to cover by 3 inches. Drain.

In a medium-size saucepan, combine the peas with water to cover by 3 inches. Bring to a boil over medium heat, skimming any foam that rises to the surface. Stir in the garlic and bay leaves. Reduce the heat, partially cover, and simmer, for about 40 minutes, or until the peas are tender; stir occasionally and add water if necessary to keep the peas covered. Drain, reserving the cooking liquid. Discard the bay leaves, and set the peas aside.

In a large heavy-bottomed saucepan, heat the vegetable oil over medium heat. Add the sausage and cook, stirring occasionally, for about 4 minutes. With a spatula, remove the sausage to a plate and set aside.

Add the onion to the saucepan and cook, stirring frequently, for about 7 minutes, or until softened. Add the bell pepper and cook for 5 minutes, or until softened. Stir in the rice, thyme, and salt.

Add water to the reserved cooking liquid to equal 1¾ cups, and stir into the rice, with the sausage. Bring to a boil, reduce the heat, and simmer, covered, for 15 minutes, or until the rice is almost tender. Stir in the peas and cook for 5 to 10 minutes, or until the rice is tender. Remove from the heat. Stir in the olive oil and vinegar. Arrange the arugula on plates and top with the beans.

¾ cup dried black-eyed peas, picked over & rinsed

3 garlic cloves, crushed

2 bay leaves, preferably Turkish

2 teaspoons vegetable oil

3 ounces andouille sausage, chorizo, or pepperoni, diced

1 large onion, coarsely chopped

1 medium-size green bell pepper, cored, seeded & diced

¾ cup Texmati, basmati, or other fragrant rice

1 tablespoon chopped fresh thyme or 1 teaspoon dried

¾ teaspoon salt

2 tablespoons olive oil

4 teaspoons sherry vinegar

2 bunches arugula, tough stems removed (3 to 4 cups)

# PORK CHOPS WITH
# PINEAPPLE & BLACK BEAN SALSA

SERVES 4

FRUIT SALSAS ARE A PERFECT ACCOMPANIMENT TO SIMPLY
BROILED, GRILLED, OR BAKED MEAT AND FISH. HERE, SMOKY BLACK
BEANS COMBINED WITH SWEET AND TANGY PINEAPPLE AND
CRISP BELL PEPPER MAKE A REFRESHING TOPPING FOR THESE JUICY
CHOPS. THE SALSA CAN BE PREPARED UP TO A DAY AHEAD.

## PINEAPPLE & BLACK BEAN SALSA

¾ cup dried black or small red chili beans

2 tablespoons fresh lime juice

1 tablespoon honey

1 small fresh or pickled jalapeño, cored, seeded & minced

1 teaspoon ground coriander

¼ teaspoon ground ginger

¾ teaspoon salt

1¼ cups diced (¼ inch) fresh or canned pineapple

1 medium-size red bell pepper, cored, seeded & cut into ½-inch dice

3 green onions, thinly sliced

3 tablespoons minced fresh cilantro

## PORK CHOPS

½ teaspoon sugar

¼ teaspoon ground coriander

¼ teaspoon ground cumin

½ teaspoon salt

⅛ teaspoon cayenne

4 (5-ounce) center-cut pork loin chops, about ¾ inch thick

Prepare the salsa: If using the chili beans, soak the beans overnight in a large bowl in water to cover by 3 inches. Drain.

In a medium-size saucepan, combine the beans with water to cover by 3 inches. Bring to a boil over medium heat, skimming any foam that rises to the surface. Reduce the heat, and simmer, partially covered, for about 1 hour, or until the beans are tender; stir occasionally and add water if necessary to keep the beans covered. Drain and set aside.

In a large bowl, whisk together the lime juice, honey, jalapeño, coriander, ginger, and salt. Stir in the beans, pineapple, bell pepper, green onions, and cilantro. Cover with plastic wrap and refrigerate.

Prepare the pork chops: Preheat the broiler, with the pan 6 inches from the heat source. In a small bowl, stir together the sugar, ground coriander, cumin, salt, and cayenne. Rub the spice mixture all over the chops.

Broil the chops for 4 to 5 minutes per side, or until browned and no longer pink in the center. Transfer the chops to warmed dinner plates and spoon salsa over them.

# ITALIAN-STYLE BAKED BEANS

GREAT NORTHERN BEANS ARE EXCELLENT FLAVOR CARRIERS. IN THIS NONTRADITIONAL VERSION OF BAKED BEANS, SLOW COOKING ALLOWS THE BEANS TO ABSORB THE FLAVORS OF ORANGE JUICE, TOMATOES, AND BASIL.

In a large bowl, soak the beans overnight in water to cover by 3 inches. Drain.

In a medium-size saucepan, combine the beans with water to cover by 3 inches. Bring to a boil over medium heat, skimming any foam that rises to the surface. Reduce the heat, partially cover, and simmer, for about 1 hour, or until the beans are tender; stir occasionally and add water if necessary to keep the beans covered. Drain the beans, reserving 2 cups of the cooking liquid. Preheat the oven to 400°F.

Cut the salt pork in half. Place half in a nonreactive 2-quart Dutch oven or bean pot and add the beans. In a medium-size bowl, combine the reserved cooking liquid, the tomatoes with their juice, the onions, basil, orange zest and juice, oregano, and garlic, and stir into the beans. Score the rind of the remaining salt pork in a crisscross fashion and bury the pork in the beans.

Cover the beans and bake 1 hour. Lower the oven temperature to 250°F. Bake, covered, for 2 hours, stirring the beans up from the bottom 2 or 3 times.

In a small bowl, combine the Parmesan and bread crumbs. Increase the oven temperature to 400°F, sprinkle the top of the beans with the bread crumb mixture, and bake, uncovered, for 30 minutes longer, or until crusty-brown on top.

1 pound Great Northern, cannellini, tongues of fire, or navy beans, picked over & rinsed

4 ounces salt pork, in one piece

1½ cups canned crushed tomatoes in juice

1 cup chopped onions

½ cup chopped fresh basil

1 teaspoon grated orange zest

¼ cup fresh orange juice

2 teaspoons minced fresh oregano or 1 teaspoon dried

6 garlic cloves, minced

⅓ cup freshly grated Parmesan cheese

¼ cup plain dried bread crumbs

# BLACK BEAN, CORN
# & WINTER SQUASH RAGOÛT

SERVES 4

THIS WINTER STEW, REDOLENT OF CINNAMON AND
CUMIN, IS REMINISCENT OF A MOLE OR A CHILI. WHILE ANISE
MAY SEEM AN UNUSUAL TOUCH, IT MARRIES WELL WITH
THE OTHER FLAVORS. SERVE THE RAGOÛT WITH A FRAGRANT
RICE SUCH AS BASMATI OR TEXMATI.

If using the chili beans, soak the beans in a medium-size bowl overnight, in water to cover by 3 inches. Drain.

In a medium-size saucepan, combine the beans with water to cover by 3 inches. Bring to a boil over medium heat, skimming any foam that rises to the surface. Reduce the heat, partially cover, and simmer, for about 1 hour, or until tender; stir occasionally and add water if necessary to keep the beans covered. Drain.

In a large nonreactive Dutch oven or heavy-bottomed saucepan, heat the oil over medium heat. Stir in the onions and garlic and cook, stirring frequently, for about 10 minutes, or until the onions are lightly golden and softened. Stir in the beans, tomatoes, 1 cup water, the oregano, anise, cinnamon, cumin, and bay leaf. Bring to a boil, reduce the heat, and simmer, partially covered, for 25 minutes.

Stir in the squash and cilantro, partially cover, and cook for 20 minutes, or until the squash and beans are tender. Add the corn and salt and cook, uncovered, for 3 to 4 minutes longer, or until the corn is tender. Remove the bay leaf and discard. Transfer the ragoût to a warmed platter and serve hot, garnished with fresh oregano sprigs, if desired.

¾ cup dried black or small red chili beans, picked over & rinsed

2 tablespoons olive oil

2 medium-size onions, cut into ½-inch chunks

4 garlic cloves, minced

1 cup chopped ripe tomatoes or canned crushed tomatoes

1¼ teaspoons dried oregano

¾ teaspoon anise seeds

¾ teaspoon cinnamon

½ teaspoon ground cumin

1 bay leaf, preferably Turkish

1 pound butternut squash, peeled, seeded & cut into 1-inch chunks

½ cup chopped fresh cilantro

1¼ cups fresh or frozen corn kernels

1 teaspoon salt

Fresh oregano sprigs, for garnish (optional)

# CURRIED BEAN, LENTIL
# & VEGETABLE STEW

SERVES 4

DESPITE ITS NAME, THE SILKY-TEXTURED, MELLOW-FLAVORED
CHINA YELLOW BEAN HAILS FROM MAINE. THOUGH TOASTING THE
CORIANDER AND CUMIN DOES BRING OUT THEIR FLAVORS,
THIS STEP IS OPTIONAL; BUT DO USE ONLY THE FRESHEST, MOST
FRAGRANT SPICES FOR THIS THICK, HEARTY STEW.

¾ cup China yellow or navy beans,
  picked over & rinsed

1 tablespoon olive oil

1 tablespoon unsalted butter

1 large onion, cut into
  1-inch chunks

3 garlic cloves, minced

2 tablespoons minced peeled
  fresh ginger

3 cups cauliflower florets

2 boiling potatoes, peeled & cut
  into 1-inch chunks

1 large carrot, sliced ½ inch thick

⅓ cup dried lentils, picked
  over & rinsed

1¼ cups chopped ripe tomatoes
  or canned crushed tomatoes

1 tablespoon plus 1 teaspoon
  ground coriander

2 teaspoons ground cumin

½ teaspoon turmeric

¼ teaspoon ground cardamom

¼ teaspoon grated nutmeg

½ teaspoon salt

¼ teaspoon freshly ground
  black pepper

⅓ cup plain low-fat yogurt

In a medium-size bowl, soak the beans overnight in water to cover by 3 inches. Drain.

In a medium-size saucepan, combine the beans with water to cover by 3 inches. Bring to a boil over medium heat, skimming any foam that rises to the surface. Reduce the heat, partially cover, and simmer, for about 1 hour, or until the beans are tender; stir occasionally and add water if necessary to keep the beans covered. Drain and set the beans aside.

In a large nonreactive Dutch oven or casserole, heat the oil and butter over medium heat. Add the onion, garlic, and ginger and cook, stirring frequently, for about 10 minutes, or until the onion is softened and golden. Add the cauliflower and cook, stirring frequently, for about 5 minutes, or until lightly colored. Add the potatoes and carrot and cook, stirring, for 2 minutes. Stir in the beans, lentils, tomatoes, and 1 cup water, and bring to a boil.

Meanwhile, in a small skillet, toast the coriander and cumin over low heat, stirring, for about 2 minutes, or until aromatic. Add to the lentil mixture along with the turmeric, cardamom, nutmeg, salt, and pepper. Stir in the yogurt, 1 tablespoon at a time. Reduce the heat and simmer, covered, for about 45 minutes, or until the lentils are tender. Spoon into warmed soup bowls.

# PORK & PINK BEAN CHILI

SERVES 4

HOT AND SPICY CHILI POWDER, ALONG WITH A TOUCH OF
COCOA POWDER, GIVES THIS CHILI ITS DEEP, FULL FLAVOR. PINK BEANS,
WITH THEIR MEALY TEXTURE, BLEND NICELY WITH THE SPICES
AND PORK SHOULDER AND COOK TO A MELTINGLY TENDER STEW. SERVE
WITH RICE OR CORN BREAD, AND PASS THE HOT SAUCE.

1 cup dried pink, red kidney,
cranberry, or small red chili
beans, picked over & rinsed

3 tablespoons all-purpose flour

1 tablespoon yellow cornmeal

1½ pounds boneless pork shoulder,
cut into 1-inch chunks

3 tablespoons olive oil

2 medium-size onions,
coarsely chopped

6 garlic cloves, minced

2 teaspoons medium-hot
chili powder

1½ teaspoons ground cumin

1 teaspoon ground coriander

1 teaspoon dried oregano

¾ teaspoon cinnamon

¾ teaspoon unsweetened
cocoa powder

1¼ cups chopped ripe
or canned tomatoes

1¼ teaspoons salt

In a large bowl, soak the beans overnight in water to cover by 3 inches. Drain.

In a medium-size saucepan, combine the beans with water to cover by 3 inches. Bring to a boil over medium heat, skimming any foam that rises to the surface. Reduce the heat, partially cover, and simmer, for about 1 hour, or until the beans are tender; stir occasionally and add water if necessary to keep the beans covered. Drain, reserving 1½ cups of the cooking liquid, and set aside.

Preheat the oven to 350°F.

On a sheet of waxed paper, stir together the flour and cornmeal. Dredge the pork in the flour mixture, shaking off the excess.

In a large nonreactive ovenproof Dutch oven, heat 2 tablespoons of the oil over medium heat. Add the pork and cook, stirring frequently, for 5 minutes, or until lightly browned. Transfer the meat to a plate.

Heat the remaining 1 tablespoon oil in the pot. Add the onions and garlic and cook, stirring frequently, for 7 minutes, or until softened. Stir in the chili powder, cumin, coriander, oregano, cinnamon, and cocoa powder and cook, stirring, for 30 seconds. Stir in the tomatoes, the reserved cooking liquid, the beans, pork, and salt. Bring to a boil. Cover, place in the oven, and bake, stirring once or twice, for 1¼ hours, or until the meat is tender. Serve.

# PINK BEANS & CHORIZO

SERVES 4

THIS LUSTY STEW IS MADE WITH CHORIZO, A SPICY
SPANISH SAUSAGE. IF CHORIZO IS UNAVAILABLE, SUBSTITUTE A
GOOD-QUALITY GARLIC SAUSAGE. SERVE PINK BEANS &
CHORIZO AS AN ENTREE; FRESH-BAKED, CUSTARDY CORNBREAD
WOULD BE AN INSPIRED ACCOMPANIMENT.

In a large bowl, soak the beans overnight in water to cover by 3 inches. Drain and set the beans aside.

In a medium-size nonreactive saucepan, heat 2 teaspoons of the oil over low heat. Add the onions and cook, stirring frequently, for about 7 minutes, or until softened and lightly colored. Add the remaining 1 teaspoon oil and the bell pepper, stirring to coat, and cook, stirring, for 3 minutes. Stir in the tomatoes and cook for 2 minutes, or until the liquid is slightly reduced. Add the beans, 2½ cups water, and marjoram. Bring to a boil. Reduce the heat, cover, and simmer, stirring occasionally, for 1 hour.

Add the chorizo, raisins, and olives. Cover and cook for 30 minutes longer, or until the beans are tender. Stir in the almonds, parsley, salt, and pepper and cook for 5 minutes. Spoon into warmed bowls.

1 cup dried pink, red kidney, or cranberry beans, picked over & rinsed

1 tablespoon olive oil

2 medium-size onions, cut into ½-inch dice

1 medium-size green bell pepper, cored, seeded & cut into ½-inch dice

¾ cup canned crushed tomatoes

¾ teaspoon dried marjoram

2 (3-ounce) chorizo, sliced ¼ inch thick

⅓ cup seedless dark raisins

¼ cup pitted green olives, coarsely chopped

¼ cup whole natural unblanched almonds, coarsely chopped

¼ cup chopped fresh flat-leaf parsley

½ teaspoon salt

¼ teaspoon freshly ground black pepper

# PAPPARDELLE CATALAN-STYLE

PICADA, THE ALMOND-BASED THICKENING AND FLAVORING
AGENT USED IN THE CATALONIA REGION OF SPAIN, GIVES BODY AND
SOUL TO THIS PASTA SAUCE. WITH THEIR NUTTY QUALITY,
CHICK-PEAS MARRY WELL WITH THE GUTSY FLAVORS OF THE PICADA
AND LEND A MEATINESS TO THE DISH.

½ cup dried chick-peas,
  picked over & rinsed


PICADA

2 tablespoons extra-virgin olive oil

2 garlic cloves, slivered

2 slices crusty bread, about 1 inch
  thick, cut into large cubes

¼ cup whole natural
  unblanched almonds

¼ cup chopped flat-leaf parsley


PASTA SAUCE

2 tablespoons olive oil

2 large onions

4 garlic cloves, minced

½ teaspoon sugar

1 medium-size poblano pepper

1 (28-ounce) can crushed
  tomatoes in juice

1½ cups chicken broth

½ teaspoon hot pepper flakes

½ teaspoon salt

¼ teaspoon freshly ground
  black pepper

Large pinch of saffron


10 ounces pappardelle

In a medium-size bowl, soak the chick-peas overnight in water to cover by 3 inches. Drain.

In a medium-size saucepan, combine the chick-peas with water to cover by 3 inches. Bring to a boil, skimming any foam that rises to the surface. Reduce the heat and simmer, partially covered, for about 1½ hours, or until the chick-peas are tender; stir occasionally and add water if necessary to keep the chick-peas covered. Drain and set aside.

Prepare the picada: In a large skillet, heat the oil over low heat. Add the garlic and cook, stirring, for 1 minute, or until fragrant. Add the bread cubes and almonds and cook, stirring frequently, for about 4 minutes, or until the bread cubes are golden.

Transfer the garlic mixture to a food processor fitted with the metal blade and process until finely ground. Transfer to a small bowl. Stir in the parsley and set aside.

Prepare the sauce: Cut the onions into 1-inch chunks. In a very large skillet or Dutch oven, heat the oil over low heat. Add the onions and garlic, sprinkle with the sugar, and cook, stirring frequently, for about 20 minutes, or until the onions are golden brown and caramelized.

With a small sharp knife, core and seed the pepper and cut into ½-inch dice. Stir the pepper

into the onion mixture and cook for 3 to 4 minutes, or until almost tender. Stir in the tomatoes with their juice and the broth and cook for 5 minutes.

Stir in the chick-peas, hot pepper flakes, salt, black pepper, and saffron. Bring to a boil over medium heat, reduce the heat, cover, and simmer for 15 minutes. Uncover and simmer 10 minutes longer, or until the sauce lightly coats a spoon.

Meanwhile, bring a large pot of water to a boil. Cook the pappardelle according to the package directions until al dente, firm but tender. Drain and transfer to a large, warmed serving bowl. Toss the hot cooked pasta with the sauce and sprinkle with the picada. Serve immediately.

*Pappardelle Catalan-Style (overleaf)*

# CHILES RELLENOS

TYPICALLY MADE WITH SMOKY POBLANO PEPPERS,
CHILES RELLENOS ARE BATTER-DIPPED AND FRIED. THIS VERSION
USES READILY AVAILABLE GREEN BELL PEPPERS, CORED
AND STUFFED WITH CHEESE AND GENTLY HEATED IN A COMPLEX
SAUCE OF BEANS, FRUITS, AND SPICES.

¼ cup dried small red chili,
    red kidney, pink, appaloosa,
    or anasazi beans, picked
    over & rinsed

¼ cup dried black beans, picked
    over & rinsed

1 tablespoon corn or other
    vegetable oil

1 large onion, halved lengthwise
    & thinly sliced crosswise

3 garlic cloves, slivered

3 tablespoons sesame seeds

2 tablespoons whole natural
    unblanched almonds

½ cup chopped ripe tomatoes or
    canned crushed tomatoes

1 small banana, peeled &
    thinly sliced

½ cup pitted prunes

¼ cup coarsely broken dried
    pasilla chile peppers or
    1 small green chile pepper,
    cored, seeded & chopped

¾ teaspoon dried oregano

½ teaspoon cinnamon

3 tablespoons red wine vinegar

1¼ teaspoons salt

4 large green bell peppers

3 cups shredded Monterey
    or pepper Jack cheese

In a medium-size bowl, soak the beans overnight in water to cover by 3 inches. Drain and set the beans aside.

In a large nonreactive Dutch oven or casserole, heat the oil over low heat. Add the onion and garlic and cook, stirring frequently, for about 15 minutes, or until lightly golden. Add the sesame seeds and almonds and cook, stirring frequently, for about 4 minutes, or until the seeds are lightly golden. Stir in the tomatoes, banana, prunes, pasilla peppers, beans, and 4½ cups water. Bring to a boil, reduce the heat, cover, and simmer for about 1½ hours, or until the beans are very tender.

Working in batches if necessary, transfer the bean mixture to a food processor fitted with the metal blade and process to a purée. Set a coarse-mesh strainer over a large nonreactive skillet. Pour the bean mixture into the strainer and push through with the back of a spoon. Discard the solids. Stir the oregano, cinnamon, vinegar, and salt into the purée, and pour the purée into a small skillet.

Meanwhile, remove the tops from the peppers and reserve. Remove the seeds and ribs from the bell peppers. Remove a thin slice from the bottom of each pepper so that they will stand upright. In a large pot of boiling water, blanch the peppers and their tops for about 5 minutes, or until crisp-tender.

Place the peppers cut side down on paper towels to drain. When cool enough to handle, pack ¾ cup Monterey or Pepper Jack into each pepper. Replace the pepper tops and secure each with a toothpick.

Place the peppers on top of the bean purée in the skillet and cover loosely with foil. Heat over low heat for 5 to 10 minutes, or until the cheese has melted. Transfer the peppers to warmed serving plates. Remove and discard the toothpicks and spoon the sauce around the peppers.

# BOW-TIE PASTA WITH SHIITAKE MUSHROOMS & WHITE BEAN SAUCE

SERVES 4

GREAT NORTHERN BEANS REMAIN FIRM WHEN
COOKED BUT CAN BE EASILY MASHED TO THICKEN A PASTA
SAUCE OR A SOUP. PAIRED WITH THE SHIITAKE
MUSHROOMS, THE BEANS CREATE A WOODSY FLAVOR IN
THIS VEGETARIAN DISH.

¾ cup dried Great Northern
or cannellini beans, picked
over & rinsed

½ ounce dried shiitake mushrooms

2 tablespoons olive oil

8 ounces fresh shiitake mushrooms,
wiped clean, stemmed
& sliced ½-inch thick

4 garlic cloves, minced

1 pound ripe tomatoes,
peeled & chopped

⅓ cup packed coarsely
chopped fresh basil

1 teaspoon salt

½ teaspoon freshly ground
black pepper

10 ounces bow-tie pasta

Fresh basil, for garnish (optional)

In a large bowl, soak the beans overnight in water to cover by 3 inches. Drain.

In a medium-size saucepan, combine the beans with water to cover by 3 inches. Bring to a boil over medium heat, skimming any foam that rises to the surface. Reduce the heat, partially cover, and simmer, for about 1 hour, or until tender; stir occasionally and add water if necessary to keep the beans covered. Drain, reserving 1 cup of the cooking liquid, and set the beans aside.

Meanwhile, in a small bowl, combine the dried mushrooms and 1 cup boiling water and let stand for 30 minutes, or until softened. Then lift the mushrooms from the soaking liquid, rinse to remove any grit, and slice ¼ inch thick. Strain the soaking liquid into a bowl through a fine-mesh sieve lined with cheesecloth or a dampened paper towel and set aside.

In a large nonreactive skillet, heat the oil over medium heat. Add the fresh mushrooms and cook, stirring frequently, for about 5 minutes, or until softened. Add the garlic and dried mushrooms and cook, stirring frequently, for 2 to 3 minutes, or until the garlic is softened. Add the tomatoes and cook for about 4 minutes, or until the mixture has thickened slightly. Stir in the beans, the reserved bean cooking liquid and mushroom soaking liquid, the basil, salt,

and pepper. Bring to a boil. Reduce the heat, crush
about ⅓ cup of the beans, and simmer for 5 to 7
minutes, or until the sauce is slightly thickened.

Meanwhile, cook the pasta according to the
package directions until al dente, firm but tender.
Drain the pasta. Transfer to a large, warmed serving
bowl. Toss the sauce with the hot cooked pasta,
and serve garnished with fresh basil, if desired.

*Bow-tie Pasta with Shiitake*
*Mushrooms & White Bean Sauce (overleaf)*

# CHOLENT

SERVES 8

ALTHOUGH STEEPED IN JEWISH TRADITION, THE RECIPE FOR
CHOLENT VARIES FROM COUNTRY TO COUNTRY; THIS ONE IS A COMBINATION
OF MOROCCAN AND HUNGARIAN INFLUENCES. ORTHODOX
LAW FORBIDS COOKING DURING THE SABBATH, AND THIS MEAL CAN BE
PREPARED AHEAD AND KEPT WARM OVER A VERY LOW FLAME.

⅔ cup dried white kidney beans,
   picked over & rinsed

⅔ cup dried baby or large lima
   beans, picked over & rinsed

2 tablespoons corn oil

3 pounds well-trimmed short ribs
   of beef, cut ¾ inch thick
   & 3 inches long

2 large onions, chopped

5 garlic cloves, slivered

2 carrots, thinly sliced

2 parsnips, peeled & thinly sliced

1½ teaspoons sweet paprika

1 teaspoon ground ginger

1 teaspoon sugar

¾ teaspoon ground cinnamon

¾ teaspoon dried thyme

¼ teaspoon ground cloves

½ teaspoon freshly ground
   black pepper

½ cup pitted prunes,
   coarsely chopped

3 tablespoons pearl barley

1 large boiling potato, peeled &
   cut into ½-inch chunks

1 sweet potato, peeled & cut into
   ½-inch chunks

1½ teaspoons salt

Chopped fresh flat-leaf parsley

In a large bowl, soak the beans overnight in water to cover by 3 inches. Drain.

In a medium-size saucepan, combine the beans with water to cover by 3 inches. Bring to a boil over medium heat; skim any foam that rises to the surface. Reduce the heat, partially cover, and simmer, for about 1 hour, or until tender; stir occasionally and add water if necessary to keep the beans covered. Drain.

Preheat the oven to 350°F.

In a large ovenproof Dutch oven or casserole, heat 1 tablespoon of the oil over medium heat. Add half the ribs and cook for about 3 minutes per side, or until browned. Remove to a bowl and repeat with the remaining oil and meat.

Add the onions and garlic to the oil remaining in the pot and cook, stirring frequently, for about 7 minutes, or until the onions are softened. Stir in the carrots and parsnips and cook, stirring frequently, for about 5 minutes, or until softened. Stir in the paprika, ginger, sugar, cinnamon, thyme, cloves, and pepper. Stir in 4½ cups water, then stir in the prunes, barley, beans, and ribs, and bring to a boil. Cover, place in the oven, and bake for 1½ hours, or until the meat is almost tender.

Stir in the potato, sweet potato, and salt and bake, covered, for 1 hour, or until the ingredients are tender. Sprinkle with parsley and serve.

# RISOTTO WITH RED BEANS

SERVES 4

RISOTTOS, WHICH ARE RICH BY NATURE, ARE OFTEN
SUBTLY FLAVORED. HERE, THOUGH, RED BEANS AND BEEF BROTH
BRING A ROBUST DEPTH TO THE DISH. SERVE RISOTTO
AS A MAIN COURSE, WITH A COOL, CRUNCHY SALAD SUCH AS
GREEN BEANS VINAIGRETTE.

In a large bowl, soak the beans overnight in water to cover by 3 inches. Drain.

In a medium-size saucepan, combine the beans with water to cover by 3 inches. Bring to a boil over medium heat, skimming any foam that rises to the surface. Reduce the heat, partially cover, and simmer, for about 1 hour, or until tender; stir occasionally and add water if necessary to keep the beans covered. Drain and set the beans aside.

In a large nonreactive heavy-bottomed saucepan, heat the butter and oil over low heat. Add the onion and cook, stirring frequently, for 15 to 20 minutes, or until the onion is very tender and golden. Meanwhile, in a medium-size saucepan, bring the beef broth to a bare simmer. Add the rice to the onion, stirring to coat, and cook for about 2 minutes, or until chalky-white. Add the wine and cook, stirring, for about 3 minutes, or until the wine has evaporated.

Stir ½ cup broth into the rice and cook, stirring, until all the broth has been absorbed. Stir in another ½ cup broth and continue stirring and adding broth until the rice is creamy and just tender, but not mushy, about 35 minutes in all. Stirring vigorously, add the beans, Fontina, salt, and pepper. Spoon onto warmed plates and serve immediately.

½ cup dried small red chili beans, picked over & rinsed

1 tablespoon unsalted butter

2 teaspoons olive oil

1 large onion, finely chopped

3½ cups beef broth

1¼ cups Arborio rice

½ cup dry red wine

1 cup shredded Italian Fontina cheese

½ teaspoon salt

¼ teaspoon freshly ground black pepper

*Risotto with Red Beans (overleaf)*

# ROAST CHICKEN WITH ORZO & CHICK-PEA STUFFING

SERVES 4

IN THIS STUFFING THE NUTTINESS AND PLEASANTLY MEALY
TEXTURE OF THE CHICK-PEAS MARRY WELL WITH THE CREAMY ORZO
AND SHARP LEMON FLAVOR OF THE ZEST AND JUICE. SUN-DRIED
TOMATOES AND PINE NUTS GIVE MORE OF A FLAVOR PUNCH, WHILE
SPINACH PROVIDES A MELLOW COUNTERPOINT.

### ORZO & CHICK-PEA STUFFING

½ cup dried chick-peas, picked over & rinsed

¼ cup pine nuts

¾ cup orzo

3 garlic cloves, minced

4 ounces spinach, stemmed & shredded

⅓ cup chopped drained sun-dried tomatoes packed in oil

3 tablespoons unsalted butter, at room temperature

1 teaspoon grated lemon zest

3 tablespoons fresh lemon juice

1 teaspoon salt

½ teaspoon freshly ground black pepper

1 (3½ pound) chicken, rinsed & dried

½ cup chicken broth

Prepare the stuffing: In a medium-size bowl, soak the chick-peas overnight in water to cover by 3 inches. Drain.

In a small heavy skillet, toast the pine nuts over medium heat, shaking the skillet occasionally, for 2 to 3 minutes, or until lightly golden. Cool and set aside.

In a medium-size saucepan, combine the chick-peas with water to cover by 3 inches. Bring to a boil over medium heat, skimming any foam that rises to the surface. Reduce the heat, partially cover, and simmer, for about 1½ hours, or until tender; stir occasionally and add water if necessary to keep the chick-peas covered. Drain and set aside.

Cook the orzo according to the package directions until al dente, firm but tender; add the garlic to the pot about 1 minute before the orzo is cooked. Drain and transfer the orzo to a large bowl.

Add the spinach to the hot cooked orzo, stirring until it is wilted. Stir in the sun-dried tomatoes, pine nuts, 2 tablespoons of the butter, the lemon zest, 2 tablespoons of the lemon juice, ¾ teaspoon of the salt, the pepper, and chick-peas. Let cool completely.

Preheat the oven to 400°F.

Sprinkle the inside of the chicken with the remaining 1 tablespoon lemon juice and ¼ teaspoon salt. With your fingers, separate the skin of the breast from the meat. Rub the remaining

1 tablespoon butter under the skin. Stuff the chicken with 2½ cups of the stuffing. With kitchen string, tie the ends of the drumsticks together, and loop string around the wings and body to hold the wings against the chicken.

Place the chicken, breast side up in a roasting pan, and roast for 45 minutes.

Spoon the remaining orzo stuffing into a small baking pan, pour the broth over, cover with foil, and place in the oven alongside the chicken. Continue to roast for another 30 minutes, or until the chicken skin is golden brown, the meat is no longer pink near the leg bone, and the stuffing in the pan is heated through. Let the chicken stand for 10 minutes, then remove the stuffing from the cavity and carve the chicken into serving portions. Serve with the stuffing.

# ASIAN-SEASONED PORK STEW WITH SOYBEANS

SERVES 4

SOYBEANS READILY ABSORB THE FLAVORS OF THE DISH
IN WHICH THEY ARE COOKED AND CONTRIBUTE A SLIGHT CRUNCH,
SIMILAR TO THAT OF PEANUTS. A FRAGRANT RICE SUCH
AS BASMATI, TEXMATI, OR JASMINE IS THE PERFECT ACCOMPANIMENT
TO THIS EASILY ASSEMBLED STEW.

BEANS

¾ cup dried soybeans, picked over & rinsed

½ cup sliced green onions

3 garlic cloves, minced

1 tablespoon peeled minced fresh ginger

PORK

⅓ cup hoisin sauce

2 tablespoons ketchup

1 teaspoon brown sugar

½ teaspoon Asian chile paste

1½ pounds boneless pork shoulder, cut into 1-inch chunks

⅓ cup packed chopped fresh cilantro

¼ cup minced green onions

2 garlic cloves, minced

1 tablespoon minced peeled fresh ginger

2 strips orange zest, 3 by ½ inch

¼ teaspoon salt

2 medium-size red bell peppers, cored, seeded & cut into strips

2 carrots, thinly sliced

Prepare the beans: In a large bowl, soak the beans overnight in water to cover by 3 inches. Drain.

In a medium-size saucepan, combine the beans with water to cover by 3 inches. Bring to a boil over medium heat, skimming any foam that rises to the surface. Reduce the heat and stir in the green onions, garlic, and ginger. Partially cover and simmer, for about 2 hours, or until the beans are tender; stir occasionally and add water if necessary to keep the beans covered. Drain and set the beans aside.

Meanwhile, prepare the pork: In a large heavy saucepan or Dutch oven, stir together the hoisin sauce, ketchup, sugar, and chile paste over medium heat. Add the pork and stir to coat. Add 1½ cups water, the cilantro, green onions, garlic, ginger, orange zest, and salt and bring to a boil. Reduce the heat and simmer, covered, for 1 hour.

Stir the beans into the stew and return to a boil. Reduce the heat and simmer, covered, for 20 minutes, or until the meat is tender. Stir in the bell peppers and carrots and return to a boil. Reduce the heat and simmer, covered, for 20 minutes, or until the vegetables are tender and the sauce is glossy and thickened. Serve with rice.

# FEIJOADA

SERVES 8 TO 10

IN A SCALED-DOWN VERSION OF THE EXTRAVAGANT
BRAZILIAN NATIONAL DISH, THE SPICY MEAT-AND-BEANS ARE BALANCED
WITH COOLING CITRUS SALADS. FEIJOADA IS DEFINITELY PARTY
FARE, ESPECIALLY AT BANQUETS. THE BEANS, HOT SAUCE, AND ORANGE
SALAD MAY EACH BE PREPARED A DAY IN ADVANCE.

### BEANS

1¾ cups dried black beans, picked
   over & rinsed

1 large red bell pepper, cored,
   seeded & diced

1 large onion, coarsely chopped

⅔ cup chopped ripe tomatoes or
   canned crushed tomatoes

5 garlic cloves, crushed

2 bay leaves, preferably Turkish

1¾ teaspoons dried oregano

1¾ teaspoons dried tarragon

### MEAT

3 tablespoons fresh orange juice

2 tablespoons sugar

1 teaspoon dried oregano

1 teaspoon salt

½ teaspoon hot pepper flakes

2 pounds meaty country-style
   pork spareribs

1½ pounds boneless beef shin or
   chuck, in 1 or 2 pieces

8 ounces slab bacon, in 1 piece,
   rind removed

1 tablespoon corn or other
   vegetable oil

2 (3-ounce) chorizo

Prepare the beans: In a large nonreactive pot, combine the beans and 8 cups water and bring to a boil, skimming any foam that rises to the surface. Add the bell pepper, onion, tomatoes, garlic, bay leaves, oregano, and tarragon, and return to a boil. Reduce the heat, cover, and simmer for 1½ hours, or until the beans are tender.

Meanwhile, prepare the meat: In a large non-reactive bowl, stir together the orange juice, sugar, oregano, ½ teaspoon salt, and hot pepper flakes. Add all the meat, and turn to coat. Marinate for 30 minutes to 1 hour at room temperature.

In a large nonreactive skillet, heat the oil over medium heat. Working in batches, add the marinated meats and sauté for about 4 minutes per side, until browned and lightly caramelized. Transfer to a plate.

When the beans are tender, add the sautéed meats to the pot and return to a boil. Stir in the remaining ½ teaspoon salt. Reduce the heat, cover, and simmer for 1½ hours. Add the chorizo and cook for 30 minutes longer, or until all the meats are tender and cooked through. Remove from the heat.

Meanwhile, prepare the salad: Place the onion slices in a bowl with ice water to cover. Let stand for 30 minutes. Drain, pat dry, and place in a bowl.

With a paring knife, remove the skin and white pith from the oranges. Separate into segments, discarding the membranes, and add to the onion slices. Stir in the oil, vinegar, and salt and set aside.

Prepare the sauce: Remove the papery husks, rinse, and pat dry. Broil or, using tongs, hold over a gas flame, turning them as they char, for about 4 minutes. When cool enough to handle, peel and chop the tomatillos. In a small serving bowl, whisk together the lime juice and oil. Stir in the tomatillos or tomatoes, the jalapeño, sugar, salt, and hot pepper flakes. Set aside.

In a medium-size saucepan, bring 3 cups water to a boil over medium heat. Stir in the rice and salt, reduce the heat, cover, and simmer, for 17 to 20 minutes, or until the rice is just tender. Transfer the rice to a serving bowl and keep warm.

In a large skillet, heat the oil over medium heat. Add the kale, sprinkle with the salt, and cook, stirring, for about 3 minutes, or until tender and heated through. Transfer to a serving bowl to keep warm.

To serve, remove the bay leaves from the beans and discard. Remove the meats from the beans, slice, and place on a large platter. Spoon some of the cooking liquid over the meat. Spoon the beans and the remaining cooking liquid into a serving bowl. Arrange the salad, rice, hot pepper sauce, and kale in bowls around the platter. Serve each guest some of everything.

ORANGE SALAD

1 medium-size red onion, halved
   lengthwise & thinly sliced
   crosswise

6 navel oranges

3 tablespoons olive oil

1 tablespoon red wine vinegar

¼ teaspoon salt

LIME & HOT PEPPER SAUCE

4 tomatillos or ¼ cup chopped
   ripe tomatoes

¼ cup fresh lime juice

1 tablespoon olive oil

1 jalapeño, cored,
   seeded & chopped

1 teaspoon sugar

¼ teaspoon salt

⅛ to ¼ teaspoon hot pepper flakes

1½ cups basmati, jasmine,
   or long-grain white rice

¼ teaspoon salt

2 teaspoons olive oil

2 bunches kale, stemmed, torn into
   bite-size pieces & blanched

⅛ teaspoon salt

# LAMB WITH ARTICHOKES
# & FLAGEOLETS

SERVES 4

DELICATE IN BOTH FLAVOR AND COLOR, FLAGEOLETS
ARE GENERALLY CULTIVATED IN FRANCE AND IMPORTED TO THE
UNITED STATES. THE PAIRING OF FLAGEOLETS AND LAMB IS
A TRADITIONAL ONE, AND HERE IN A DISH PERFECT FOR SPRING,
ARTICHOKES AND SHALLOTS SEASON THE MIX.

½ cup dried flageolet, cannellini, or Great Northern beans, picked over & rinsed

2 tablespoons olive oil

1¼ pounds boneless lamb shoulder, cut into 1-inch chunks

3 tablespoons all-purpose flour

12 shallots, peeled

8 large garlic cloves

⅔ cup dry red wine

⅔ cup chopped ripe tomatoes or canned crushed tomatoes

1 tablespoon chopped fresh tarragon or 1 teaspoon dried

8 medium-size artichokes

¾ teaspoon salt

1 tablespoon balsamic vinegar

2 tablespoons chopped fresh flat-leaf parsley

In a medium-size bowl, soak the beans overnight in water to cover by 3 inches. Drain.

In a medium-size saucepan, combine the beans with water to cover by 3 inches. Bring to a boil over medium heat, skimming any foam that rises to the surface. Reduce the heat, partially cover, and simmer, for 30 minutes; stir occasionally and add water if necessary to keep the beans covered. Drain and set the beans aside.

Preheat the oven to 350°F.

In a large nonreactive ovenproof Dutch oven or casserole, heat the oil over medium heat. Dredge the lamb in the flour, shaking off the excess, and add to the pot. Cook, stirring frequently, for about 5 minutes, or until lightly browned. Transfer the lamb to a plate.

Reduce the heat to low, add the shallots and garlic, and cook, stirring frequently, for about 5 minutes, or until golden brown.

Increase the heat to high and add the wine, stirring up any browned bits from the bottom of the pot. Boil for 4 minutes, or until reduced by about half. Return the lamb to the pot along with 1 cup water, tomatoes, tarragon, and beans. Bring to a boil. Cover the pot, place in the oven, and bake for 40 minutes.

Meanwhile, remove the leaves from the artichokes and save to steam for other dishes.

Remove the chokes. Peel the stems, leaving them attached to the artichoke hearts. Slice the hearts with stems in half lengthwise.

Stir the artichoke hearts into the pot, cover, and bake for 30 minutes longer, or until the meat, beans, and artichokes are tender. Stir in the salt, vinegar, and parsley. Spoon onto warmed dinner plates and serve.

# RICE & BEAN CAKE

SERVES 8

SLIGHTLY CRUNCHY ON THE OUTSIDE, CREAMY WITHIN,

A SLICE OF THIS RICE CAKE SERVED ON A TANGY ARUGULA SALAD

MAKES AN ELEGANT APPETIZER OR SIDE DISH. FOR A PARTY,

THE CAKE MAY BE MADE AHEAD, THEN GENTLY REHEATED IN A LOW

OVEN BEFORE SERVING AS PART OF A BUFFET.

⅔ cup dried cranberry or pinto
  beans, picked over & rinsed

3 tablespoons olive oil

4 garlic cloves, minced

2 teaspoons grated lemon zest

¾ teaspoon dried sage or
  1½ teaspoons fresh sage,
  chopped

1 teaspoon salt

2 tablespoons unsalted butter

1 large onion, finely chopped

1¼ cups long-grain white rice

1¼ cups chicken broth

¼ teaspoon freshly ground
  black pepper

2 tablespoons fresh lemon juice

2 tablespoons plain dried
  bread crumbs

¾ cup freshly grated Pecorino
  Romano or Parmesan cheese

¾ cup shredded mozzarella cheese

1 large egg plus 1 large egg yolk

In a medium-size bowl, soak the beans overnight in water to cover by 3 inches. Drain.

In a medium-size saucepan, stir together the beans, 2½ cups water, the oil, the garlic, ¾ teaspoon of the lemon zest, and the sage. Bring to a boil over medium heat, skimming any foam that rises to the surface. Reduce the heat, and simmer, partially covered, for about 1½ hours, or until the beans are very tender; stir occasionally and add water if necessary to keep the beans covered. Drain and reserve the cooking liquid.

In a medium-size bowl, stir together the beans and ½ teaspoon of the salt. Set aside.

In a medium-size saucepan, melt the butter over low heat. Add the onion and cook, stirring frequently, for about 15 minutes, or until the onion is softened and golden. Add the rice, stirring to coat with the butter. In a liquid measuring cup, combine the reserved bean cooking liquid and enough broth to equal 2¾ cups. Stir the broth mixture into the rice along with the remaining 1¼ teaspoons lemon zest, ½ teaspoon salt, and the pepper. Bring to a boil, reduce the heat, cover, and simmer for about 17 minutes, or until the rice is tender. Transfer to a bowl, stir in the lemon juice, and cool to room temperature.

Preheat the oven to 350°F. Generously butter an 8- by 1½-inch round cake pan. Sprinkle the pan with the bread crumbs to coat.

Stir the Pecorino Romano or Parmesan, mozzarella, egg, and egg yolk into the cooled rice mixture. Spoon half the rice mixture into the prepared pan, patting it down. Spoon the beans over the top, spreading them almost to the edge of the pan. Spoon the remaining rice mixture over the beans, patting it down and smoothing the top. Butter a sheet of foil and place buttered side down on the rice.

Bake for about 35 minutes, or until the rice cake is set. Increase the oven temperature to 475°F, uncover the pan, and bake for 20 minutes longer, or until the top is crusty. Let cool for 10 minutes. Run a metal spatula around the edge of the pan and turn the cake out onto a serving plate.

*Rice & Bean Cake (overleaf)*

# SPICY MOONG DAL

MOONG DAL, WHICH IS THE DRIED, HULLED, AND SPLIT
MUNG BEAN, CAN BE FOUND IN INDIAN AND CHINESE MARKETS. IT IS
SIMILAR TO SPLIT PEAS, WITH A SLIGHTLY SWEET, NUTTY TASTE
AND A GRANULAR TEXTURE. THE ONION GARNISH IN THIS DISH IS A
SPICY COUNTERPOINT TO THE MELLOW DAL.

DAL

1 cup moong dal, picked
   over & rinsed

1 large medium-tart apple, such as
   MacIntosh or Empire, peeled,
   cored & thinly sliced (1 cup)

2 garlic cloves, peeled & slivered

3 tablespoons unsalted butter

¾ teaspoon turmeric

¾ teaspoon salt

ONION GARNISH

3 tablespoons unsalted butter

¾ teaspoon yellow mustard seeds

¼ teaspoon ground cardamom

⅛ teaspoon cayenne

2 medium-size red onions, halved
   & thinly sliced (1½ cups)

½ teaspoon sugar

Prepare the dal: In a large Dutch oven or heavy saucepan, combine 4 cups water, moong dal, apple, garlic, butter, and turmeric. Bring to a boil over medium heat, skimming any foam that rises to the surface. Reduce the heat and simmer, stirring frequently, for about 50 minutes, or until the mixture has become a thick porridge. Remove from the heat and stir in the salt.

Prepare the onion garnish: In a large skillet heat the butter over medium-high heat until bubbly. Add the mustard seeds, cardamom, and cayenne and cook for about 20 seconds, stirring constantly. Add the onions, sprinkle with the sugar, and cook, stirring almost constantly, for 5 to 7 minutes, or until the onions caramelize. Transfer the dal to a serving bowl, spoon the onion over the dal, and serve.

# REFRIED BEANS

SERVES 4

REFRIED BEANS ARE DELICIOUS WITH CHIPS
AND SALSA, AS A SIDE DISH WITH BARBECUE, OR AS PART OF
A BURRITO. TO RETAIN A CHUNKY TEXTURE, MASH
THE BEANS WITH A POTATO MASHER RATHER THAN PURÉEING
THEM IN A FOOD PROCESSOR.

In a large bowl, soak the beans overnight in water to cover by 3 inches. Drain.

In a medium-size saucepan, combine the beans with water to cover by 3 inches. Bring to a boil over medium heat, skimming any foam that rises to the surface. Stud the onion with the cloves and add to the saucepan along with the thyme, crushed garlic, and cinnamon. Reduce the heat, partially cover, and simmer, for about 1½ hours, or until the beans are very tender; stir occasionally and add water if necessary to keep the beans covered. Discard the onion with the cloves. Drain the beans, reserving ¼ cup of the cooking liquid.

In a large skillet, heat the oil over medium heat. Add the green onions and minced garlic and cook, stirring frequently, for about 4 minutes, or until softened. Stir in the beans, tomato paste, cumin and salt. With a potato masher or the back of a spoon, mash the beans to a thick paste. Add just enough of the reserved bean cooking liquid to soften the paste slightly. Serve hot.

1 cup dried small red chili or red kidney beans, picked over & rinsed

1 small onion

4 whole cloves

4 sprigs fresh thyme

5 garlic cloves, 3 crushed & 2 minced

½ teaspoon cinnamon

2 tablespoons olive oil

4 green onions, thinly sliced

1 tablespoon tomato paste

1 teaspoon ground cumin

1 teaspoon salt

# WHITE BEAN PIE

SIMILAR IN TEXTURE TO PUMPKIN PIE AND BEST SERVED
WARM OR AT ROOM TEMPERATURE, THIS PIE IS FLAVORED WITH THE
SWEET-SPICY SEASONINGS OF THE CARIBBEAN—GINGER,
CARDAMOM, AND ALLSPICE—WHICH ARE DELICIOUSLY TEMPERED
BY A PURÉE OF WHITE BEANS.

1⅓ cups dried cannellini or
Great Northern beans,
picked over & rinsed

CRUST

1½ cups all-purpose flour

2 teaspoons sugar

¼ teaspoon salt

6 tablespoons cold unsalted
butter, cut up

3 tablespoons solid vegetable
shortening

FILLING

2 large eggs plus 2 large egg yolks

¾ cup milk

⅔ cup heavy cream

⅔ cup sugar

2 tablespoons light corn syrup

1 teaspoon pure vanilla extract

1¼ teaspoons ground ginger

½ teaspoon ground cardamom

⅛ teaspoon ground allspice

⅛ teaspoon ground white pepper

In a large bowl, soak the beans overnight in water to cover by 3 inches. Drain.

Prepare the crust: In a large bowl, stir together the flour, sugar, and salt. With a pastry blender or 2 knives, cut in the butter and shortening until the mixture resembles coarse meal. Stir in just enough ice water for the dough to form a ball (about ⅓ cup); do not overwork. Wrap the dough in plastic wrap and refrigerate for several hours or, preferably, overnight.

Prepare the filling: In a medium-size saucepan, combine the beans with water to cover by 3 inches. Bring to a boil over medium heat, skimming any foam that rises to the surface. Reduce the heat, partially cover, and simmer, for about 1 hour, or until the beans are tender; stir occasionally and add water if necessary to keep the beans covered. Drain.

Place the beans in a food processor fitted with the metal blade and process until puréed. Push the purée through a food mill or with the back of a spoon through a medium-mesh sieve set over a bowl. Discard the skins. You should have about 2 cups of purée.

In a large bowl, whisk together the bean purée, eggs, egg yolks, milk, cream, sugar, corn syrup, vanilla, ginger, cardamom, allspice, and pepper. Cover and refrigerate.

Preheat the oven to 400°F.

On a lightly floured work surface, roll the dough out to a 13-inch round. Brush off any excess flour and carefully fit the dough into a 9-inch pie plate, forming a high fluted edge. Prick the bottom of the shell with a fork. Line with foil or wax paper and fill with dried beans or pie weights. Place on a baking sheet and bake for 15 minutes. Remove the foil and weights, prick any bubbles in the shell, and bake for 10 minutes longer, or until the shell is set and golden brown. Remove from the oven and reduce the temperature to 350°F.

Whisk the bean mixture once more to blend and pour into the prepared shell. Place on a baking sheet and bake for about 1 hour, or until the filling is just set and a toothpick inserted in the center comes out clean but not dry. Serve warm or at room temperature.

# RED BEAN ICE CREAM

MAKES 1 QUART

RED ADZUKI BEANS, WITH THEIR SWEET, NUTTY FLAVOR,
WORK WELL IN BOTH SWEET AND SAVORY DISHES. THIS RENDITION
OF RED BEAN ICE CREAM, SIMILAR TO THAT SERVED IN
JAPANESE RESTAURANTS, IS SPIKED WITH CRYSTALLIZED GINGER AND
HAS A GRAINY TEXTURE SIMILAR TO CHESTNUT PURÉE.

1 cup adzuki beans, picked
   over & rinsed

1¼ cups sugar

2½ cups milk

½ cup heavy cream

1 vanilla bean, split lengthwise

⅛ teaspoon salt

3 large egg yolks

¼ cup minced crystallized ginger

In a large bowl, soak the beans overnight in water to cover by 3 inches. Drain.

In a medium-size saucepan, combine the beans with water to cover by 3 inches. Bring to a boil over medium heat, skimming any foam that rises to the surface. Reduce the heat, partially cover, and simmer, for about 45 minutes, or until the beans are tender; stir occasionally and add water if necessary to keep the beans covered. Drain.

Place the beans in a food processor fitted with the metal blade and process to a smooth purée. Transfer to a medium-size saucepan and stir in ¾ cup of the sugar. Cook, stirring, for about 5 minutes, or until the mixture is thick, glossy, and paste-like. Remove from the heat and set aside.

In a medium-size nonreactive saucepan, heat the milk, cream, ¼ cup of the remaining sugar, the vanilla bean, and salt over low heat until bubbles appear around the edge of the pan. Meanwhile, in a small bowl, whisk together the egg yolks and the remaining ¼ cup sugar.

Gradually whisk about 1 cup of the warm milk mixture into the yolk mixture. Then whisk the yolk mixture and the bean purée into the remaining milk mixture in the saucepan. Cook over low heat, stirring, for about 12 minutes, or until the mixture coats the back of a spoon. Push the mixture

through a fine-mesh sieve with the back of a spoon and remove the vanilla bean. (If you wish, wash the vanilla bean, dry it, and place it in your sugar canister to perfume the sugar.)

Chill the mixture, then transfer to an ice cream maker and process according to the manufacturer's instructions. When the ice cream is almost frozen, add the ginger. Serve immediately in chilled bowls or transfer to a freezer container to firm.

# MEXICAN DARK CHOCOLATE BEAN CAKE

SERVES 8

THE UNDERLYING FLAVOR OF ALMONDS COMBINED WITH A HANDFUL OF
HEADY SPICES IN THIS CAKE IS MEANT TO SIMULATE MEXICAN
CHOCOLATE, WHICH IS SOLD IN IN TABLETS FLAVORED WITH CINNAMON
AND ALMONDS. MASHED BLACK BEANS ADD RICHNESS AND
MOISTNESS TO THIS SPICY CAKE. SERVE WITH VANILLA ICE CREAM.

½ cup dried black beans, picked over & rinsed

1¼ cups buttermilk

½ cup unsweetened cocoa powder

2 cups all-purpose flour

1¼ teaspoons baking powder

¾ teaspoon baking soda

2½ teaspoons cinnamon

½ teaspoon freshly ground black pepper

¼ teaspoon salt

¼ teaspoon ground allspice

¼ teaspoon cayenne

¾ cup (1½ sticks) unsalted butter, at room temperature

1 cup packed dark brown sugar

¾ cup granulated sugar

3 large eggs

1 tablespoon dark rum

½ cup finely ground whole unblanched natural almonds (about 2 ounces)

3 tablespoons confectioners' sugar

In a medium-size saucepan, combine the beans with water to cover by 3 inches. Bring to a boil over medium heat, skimming any foam that rises to the surface. Reduce the heat, partially cover and simmer, for about 1 hour, or until the beans are tender; stir occasionally and add water if necessary to keep the beans covered. Drain.

In a food processor fitted with the metal blade, combine the beans, buttermilk, and cocoa powder, and process until puréed.

Preheat the oven to 350°F. Grease and flour a 13- by 9-inch baking pan. Line the bottom of the pan with waxed paper, and grease and flour the waxed paper.

In a medium-size bowl, stir together the flour, baking powder, baking soda, cinnamon, pepper, salt, allspice, and cayenne.

In the large bowl of an electric mixer, beat the butter at medium speed until creamy. Gradually beat in the brown and granulated sugars until light and fluffy. Add the eggs 1 at a time, beating well after each addition. Beat in the rum.

Fold in the flour mixture alternately with the buttermilk mixture, beginning and ending with the flour mixture. Fold in the nuts. Spoon into the prepared pan, smoothing the top. Bake for about 45 minutes, or until a toothpick inserted in the center

comes out clean but not dry. Transfer the pan to a
wire rack to cool.

Invert the pan to unmold the cake, then turn
the cake right side up. Dust with confectioners'
sugar and serve.

*Mexican Dark Chocolate
Bean Cake (overleaf)*

# SWEET SOCCA

SERVES 4

IN THE SOUTH OF FRANCE, SOCCA ARE CRÊPES
PREPARED IN COPPER PANS AND BAKED IN WOOD-FIRED OVENS,
THEN ENJOYED AS A SAVORY MID-MORNING SNACK BY
WORKERS. THE VERSION HERE IS A SWEET COUSIN. CHICK-PEA
FLOUR IS AVAILABLE IN HEALTH FOOD STORES.

CRÊPES

¾ cup chick-pea flour

½ cup all-purpose flour

3 tablespoons sugar

⅛ teaspoon ground allspice

2 large eggs

1 cup milk

3 tablespoons unsalted butter,
    melted

2 tablespoons bourbon

1 teaspoon grated lemon zest

TOPPING

2 tablespoons sugar

½ teaspoon cinnamon

2 tablespoons fresh lemon juice

Prepare the crêpes: In a large bowl, stir together the chick-pea flour, all-purpose flour, sugar, and allspice to mix thoroughly.

In a small bowl, whisk together the eggs, milk, ½ cup water, the butter, and bourbon. Whisk the egg mixture into the flour mixture until well combined. Let stand, covered, for 1 hour at room temperature.

Strain the batter through a medium-mesh sieve into a 4-cup liquid measure; stir in the lemon zest.

Brush a 10-inch nonstick skillet with oil and heat over medium-high heat. Pour in ¼ cup of the batter, swirling the skillet to coat the bottom. Cook for about 45 seconds, or until the bottom is lightly colored and the top is bubbly. Turn the crêpe over and cook for 20 seconds longer, or until the bottom is lightly colored. Transfer to a platter and keep warm in a low oven. Repeat with the remaining batter to make a total of 12 crêpes.

Prepare the topping: In a small bowl, stir together the sugar and cinnamon and sprinkle each crêpe with ½ teaspoon cinnamon sugar. Sprinkle each crêpe with ½ teaspoon lemon juice. Serve immediately, 3 crêpes per serving.

# INDEX

# CONVERSION TABLE

## WEIGHTS

| ounces & pounds | metric equivalents |
| --- | --- |
| ¼ ounce | 7 grams |
| ⅓ ounce | 10 g |
| ½ ounce | 14 g |
| 1 ounce | 28 g |
| 1½ ounces | 42 g |
| 1¾ ounces | 50 g |
| 2 ounces | 57 g |
| 3 ounces | 85 g |
| 3½ ounces | 100 g |
| 4 ounces (¼ pound) | 114 g |
| 6 ounces | 170 g |
| 8 ounces (½ pound) | 227 g |
| 9 ounces | 250 g |
| 16 ounces (1 pound) | 464 g |

## TEMPERATURES

| °F (Fahrenheit) | °C (Celsius or Centigrade) |
| --- | --- |
| 32 (water freezes) | 0 |
| 200 | 93.3 |
| 212 (water boils) | 100 |
| 250 | 120 |
| 275 | 135 |
| 300 (slow oven) | 150 |
| 325 | 160 |
| 350 (moderate oven) | 175 |
| 375 | 190 |
| 400 (hot oven) | 205 |
| 425 | 220 |
| 450 (very hot oven) | 233 |
| 475 | 245 |
| 500 (extremely hot oven) | 260 |

## LIQUID MEASURES

| spoons & cups | metric equivalents |
| --- | --- |
| ¼ teaspoon | 1.23 mm |
| ½ teaspoon | 2.5 mm |
| ¾ teaspoon | 3.7 mm |
| 1 teaspoon | 5 mm |
| 1 dessertspoon | 10 mm |
| 1 tablespoon (3 teaspoons) | 15 mm |
| 2 tablespoons (1 ounce) | 30 mm |
| ¼ cup | 60 mm |
| ⅓ cup | 80 mm |
| ½ cup | 120 mm |
| ⅔ cup | 160 mm |
| ¾ cup | 180 mm |
| 1 cup (8 ounces) | 240 mm |
| 2 cups (1 pint) | 480 mm |
| 3 cups | 710 mm |
| 4 cups (1 quart) | 1 liter |
| 4 quarts (1 gallon) | 3¾ liters |

## LENGTH

| U.S. measurements | metric equivalents |
| --- | --- |
| ⅛ inch | 3 mm |
| ¼ inch | 6 mm |
| ⅜ inch | 1 cm |
| ½ inch | 1.2 cm |
| ¾ inch | 2 cm |
| 1 inch | 2.5 cm |
| 1¼ inches | 3.1 cm |
| 1½ inches | 3.7 cm |
| 2 inches | 5 cm |
| 3 inches | 7.5 cm |
| 4 inches | 10 cm |
| 5 inches | 12.5 cm |

## APPROXIMATE EQUIVALENTS

1 kilo is slightly more than 2 pounds
1 liter is slightly more than 1 quart
1 meter is slightly over 3 feet
1 centimeter is approximately ⅜ inch